Heart of Prayer

Heart of Prayer

African, Jewish and Biblical Prayers

Anthony J. Gittens ccsp

Collins

THE AUTHOR

Anthony Gittins CCSp trained as an anthropologist, and worked as a missionary in West Africa for eight years. He spent four years in London, lecturing at the Missionary Institute, doing retreat work with young people, and hospital ministry. He is at present Professor of Mission Theology at the Catholic Theological Union in Chicago.

Collins Liturgical Publications
187 Piccadilly, London W1V 9DA

Collins Liturgical Publications
distributed in Ireland by
Educational Company of Ireland
21 Talbot Street, Dublin 1

Collins Liturgical Australia
PO Box 3023 Sydney 2001

ISBN 0 00599841 7

© compilation 1985 Anthony Gittins C.S.Sp.
First published 1985

Typeset by John G. Eccles Printers Ltd, Inverness

Contents

To my father and mother who taught me to pray

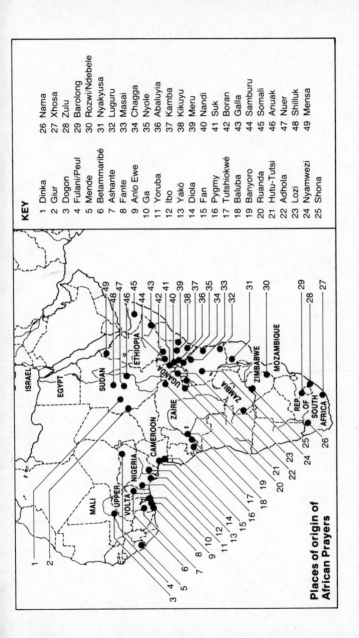

Places of origin of African Prayers

KEY

1	Dinka	26	Nama
2	Giur	27	Xhosa
3	Dogon	28	Zulu
4	Fulani/Peul	29	Barolong
5	Mende	30	Rozwi/Ndebele
6	Betammaribé	31	Nyakyusa
7	Ashante	32	Luguru
8	Fante	33	Masai
9	Anlo Ewe	34	Chagga
10	Ga	35	Nyole
11	Yoruba	36	Abaluyia
12	Ibo	37	Kamba
13	Yakö	38	Kikuyu
14	Diola	39	Meru
15	Fan	40	Nandi
16	Pygmy	41	Suk
17	Tutshiokwé	42	Boran
18	Baluba	43	Galla
19	Banyoro	44	Samburu
20	Ruanda	45	Somali
21	Hutu-Tutsi	46	Anuak
22	Adhola	47	Nuer
23	Lozi	48	Shilluk
24	Nyamwezi	49	Mensa
25	Shona		

Introduction

For those who like prayer books with formal prayers, we live in happy times; there are dozens of such books available in the shops, and they evidently supply a need. Ours is an age in which people are learning about and experimenting with many forms of prayer and of praying. Some people are helped by prayers in the form of prose or poetry, prayers with strong imagery or appeal to the senses or the social conscience; others prefer to pray straight from the heart, either with no books to assist them or with a minimum use of written prayers, and then only to stimulate them to personal reflection, meditation and union with God. Inasmuch as prayer is both communication and receptivity, *any* form of prayer which helps people in their quest for God is surely legitimate and valid.

In recent years too, there has been a noticeable and exciting rediscovery of traditions of prayer from the East and from world religions not previously very familiar to or understood by the majority of Christians.

Prayer is communion with God, whether in silence, song or shouting, whether alone or in a group. Prayer books are no more than a means to that end. Some people may feel that they are not really praying *unless* they have a prayer book; others may find that they never find a use for one. But a prayer book may be required or useful if a person finds difficulty in becoming centred in God. I myself find that though not all prayer books by any means appeal to me, nevertheless I do have quite a lot and I certainly like to pray. I also find it helpful to know something about how other people pray, and what forms of prayer they find useful. And this brings me to the present collection.

The prayers here assembled are somewhat different from most, and are offered for anyone who believes in God, anyone who wants to pray and would like some ideas, and anyone who already prays. They are, more specifically, for those who accept Jesus Christ as Saviour, and yet with a couple of exceptions they do not mention the name Jesus and do not refer to him. This is quite deliberate, and it is the characteristic feature of the prayer-book in your hands. Any prayers which have ever been said to or about Jesus are either available to us now, or are forever lost. But for Christians who want to think of God – Creator, Parent (mother or father), Protector, Healer, and so on – as understood before or independently of the Incarnation, there are many prayers in existence whose riches are virtually unknown to praying believers.

Each society has its own repository of cultural riches, and there are many cultures in which such riches are in danger of being lost or devalued as they become assimilated into the literate and computerised cultures of the modern Western scientific world. Oral traditions can survive without being written down, but only if they are transmitted verbally. If the tradition is not maintained by word of mouth, it becomes forever lost. Writing helps to preserve traditions not only among those who would otherwise forget them, but for the benefit of a wider audience. So it is that we have, in the Bible, a written record of the word of God which would otherwise have been irretrievably lost. Africa, a continent of almost unimaginable human and cultural riches, was, until recently, and like ancient Israel, a land of oral rather than of written traditions. Literacy helped destroy traditional African cultures, yet not all was lost. Many prayers and prayer-forms were collected by missionaries, anthropologists and colonial officials, and have been preserved, largely in academic or unpublished works, and are hardly available to the general reader.

This prayer book (it is not just a book of prayers but a book for praying) is offered then to all, but it has been compiled with two particular types of user in mind.

In the first place it is for Africans who are unaware of or unable to discover their own cultural heritage of prayer. The African prayers included here contain, I believe, not only an intrinsic beauty but a characteristically African style and urgency which is as redolent and evocative of authentic African worship as it is unfamiliar to the European. Whether Christian or not, Africans have a right to claim what is their own, and have every justification for taking great pride in the aspirations and formulations of their forebears. I hope that this collection will appeal to Africans as an authentic expression of indigenous worship, and be an inspiration for further reflection and meditation.

Secondly, these prayers are offered directly and with no

apology to the non-African, wherever he or she may be. Just as any culture which is unaware of its antecedents is to some extent impoverished, so any culture which cannot dip into the repository of other cultures is deprived of other perspectives and insights. Non-Africans should not remain isolated from or inured to the living tradition of prayer which, while largely unfamiliar is also refreshing and powerful.

Today, perhaps more than ever, believers must seek the unity for which Christ prayed, and one way of doing this is to pool resources and to be enriched from the stores of each other's wisdom. Africans and non-Africans, including expatriates living in Africa, should be able to discover in these prayers some universally relevant aspirations and invocations.

The Old Testament too, is a tremendous source of inspiration, long a closed book to many Christians, especially and regrettably those in the Catholic tradition. The Jewish people have mined this source for three millennia, and other believers cannot afford to neglect the Old Testament *as a source of prayer*. Yet though theologians and Scripture scholars have always quarried from this vast deposit, most of the People of God have not learned to *pray* the Old Testament, or such is my impression. The selections included here may therefore surprise some people with their power and beauty; they cannot help but speak to all of us with their inspiration.

The third component of this selection is one which I hope will be particularly helpful and new to many; it consists of prayers taken from *Forms of Prayer for Jewish Worship*, and links us with the prayers of our Jewish brothers and sisters today, for it is a contemporary Jewish prayer book. It represents a *living* tradition of prayer, just as the African prayers represent another living – though in some cases only just alive – tradition. Both traditions cry out to be shared with others; this volume puts them in the hands of all believers.

A note on the sources
The African prayers – some hundred and fifty from fifty African societies – have, obviously, been translated from other languages. In most cases they appear as they are in the sources from which I have taken them, if the sources are in English. Where the sources are in French, I have adopted a

rather free translation. And even when I have taken prayers which were in English when I found them, I have on occasion changed words, paraphrased or presented the prayers in an adapted form. The reason for this is quite simple: this is not an academic or antiquarian book, but a praying-book, and I have tried to maintain simplicity and freshness rather than slavish adherence to first-published translations. (The sources from which these prayers are taken are listed in the Bibliography, to which reference is made in the small figure following each prayer in the text.)

The Old Testament prayers, mostly Psalms, are likewise adapted whenever I have felt it appropriate. On some occasions I have retained a well-loved translation; on others I have adapted the scriptures more or less freely. Psalm 23, 'The Lord is my Shepherd', is a case in point and appears in different forms. If the ascription at the end of a prayer says the passage is *from* the Holy Bible', this should be taken to indicate the use of editorial liberty. Where the reference is simply to 'the Holy Bible', this usually indicates fidelity to the text of the Jerusalem Bible version; occasionally, some other version is used. My reason for adapting the text is simply in order to produce a simpler, less formidable, more manageable prayer. My paraphrases may not suit everyone, but the reference given will be sufficient to guide the reader/pray-er to the original source.

The prayers from the *Forms of Prayer for Jewish Worship* have been presented unchanged, with the rare exception that I have omitted 'Jewish' from the phrase 'Jewish people', to allow for a more universalistic understanding of the prayer, and I have occasionally repeated the word 'God' or an attribute of God, rather than retaining 'he'.

All the prayers in this book, but particularly the biblical and the African prayers, must be understood against their own appropriate backgrounds; they are 'traditional' prayers which speak powerfully about the earth, produce, sickness, the powers of nature, fertility, death, and other fundamental issues in worlds without nuclear bombs, genetic engineering or widespread scientific advances. These are peasant or fishing communities and their prayers are fresh and urgent and 'earthy', though directed beyond the physical earth. But they show a love for and respect of this earth, and they may remind present-day non-Africans of a dimension of prayer which might otherwise be overlooked. They have a directness and an ingenuousness, a total lack of coyness and florid style, which contrasts beautifully with many a richly decorated and sometimes sentimental prayer so familiar to European Christians. These prayers are never sentimental and often surprisingly frank. They are African and they are Israelite, and I hope they may bring all readers closer to a God who is neither remote in High Heaven nor merely a European God, but a God of all the nations, in the forests or on the savannahs as much as in the factories or in the cities.

If the imagery of some of the prayers is rather strange to Western eyes – 'God, piler-up of the great rocks', 'let not our arrows miss the animals in the bush', 'if anyone should cast a spell over us, let him die' – then we might remember that a great deal of Western Christian imagery is extremely alien to African minds; with sympathy, information and effort, things strange and alien at first sight can become illuminating and precious. A God 'robed in splendour and coming in might', or sitting on a throne judging the nations, is as much a projection of those who try to put words round God as it is incomplete and therefore distorted as it stands. Perhaps these prayers will give pause for thought and open our eyes to the tender mercies of our God too: a God who, in the words of so many Samburu prayers, and so touchingly, can respond to the requests of beloved children by saying, simply: 'All right'.

To the African, some of the unfamiliar prayers in this book may help promote a God who really does offer human beings a *developing relationship*: a notion both novel and difficult for traditional Africa. And for the European or one unfamiliar with African prayer, the Christian doctrine of the communion of saints may perhaps become more understandable through these African prayers which speak so eloquently of the essential unity of humankind and the crucial importance of group solidarity and community cooperation among all people, whether alive or dead. African prayers are closely rooted in the plight and the need of the community, even when they ask for favours for an individual; all of us can learn a lesson here.

A note on the language
Many images of God are presented in these pages; I hope they will give pause for thought. But many prayers in a more familiar style may sometimes obtrude because they uncritically reflect a male orientation in the godhead. Such prayer-

forms can be offensive, and so, wherever possible, and without destroying the imagery or flow of the prayers, I have tried to avoid sexist language, and present a universal God who loves all people (not a God who made 'man' and loves 'him': not a God who cares for 'his' people: not a God limited by our inappropriate language.)

If the male-oriented image of God is an intrinsic part of the prayer, I have sometimes left it unchanged. The person who prays these pages can of course feel free to modify the language.

A note on the structure of the book

Finally, a few remarks on the structure, presentation and possible uses of this book. There are eighteen sections, each representing a stage or life-crisis, with most of which everyone should be able to identify. All the prayers in any given section carry the theme of that section, but many could have been put in a number of different sections and they are therefore cross-indexed at the back of the book. Each prayer is discreetly numbered for ease of reference. Space has been left between prayers, and at the end of the book, again so that the reader may annotate or cross-reference the prayers or themes. Within each section the three components – Jewish, biblical, and African prayers – have been alternated in a fairly random manner and to provide variety, avoiding heavy blocks of one particular kind of prayer.

Some of the prayers are presented in straightforward prose fashion; most are offered in stanzas or sections. This is partly for cosmetic reasons, but more seriously so that two or more persons or groups may share the prayers when reading out loud. Perhaps two sides of a church or a classroom may want to alternate, or simply two readers may provide variation in voice. A further reason for presenting many prayers in sections or stanzas is so that an individual, praying privately and silently by way of meditation, may take a small section for reflection, before passing on to another image or topic. There is absolutely no need for anyone to be limited to reading these prayers straight through; they are for *praying*, and prayer takes many forms. I hope that the presentation will assist anyone – man or woman, African or European, catechist, lay leader, priest, student, or prayer-group, class, congregation and so on – to discover and enjoy walking with God in prayer.

1

The earth: God's creation

1 Creator God, we announce your goodness because it is clearly visible in the heavens where there is the light of the sun, the heat of the sun, and the light of night. There are rain clouds. The land itself shows your goodness, because it can be seen in the trees and their shade. It is clearly seen in water and grass, in the milking cows and in the cows that give us meat. Your love is visible all the time: morning and daytime, evening and night. Your love is great. It has filled the land; it has filled people. We say: 'Thank you, our God', because you have given us everything we have. You have given us our fathers and mothers, our brothers and sisters, our children and friends. You have given us cows, grass and water. We have nothing except what you have given us. You are our shield; you protect us. You are our guard; you take care of us. You are our safety, all days. You stay with us for ever and ever. You are our father and mother. Therefore we say: 'Thank you'. We worship you with our mouths. We worship you with our bodies. We worship you with everything we have, because only you have given us everything. We say: 'Thank you', today. And tomorrow. And all days. We do not tire in giving thanks to you. 27

Masai, Kenya and Tanzania

2 Yes, the greatness of God is far beyond our knowledge,
God's age is more than we can count.
Who can understand how God spreads out the clouds
or why God causes the thunder to crash so loudly?
God spreads out the mist, wrapping it round God's own
    self,
and covers the tops of the mountains.

Listen, oh listen to the blast of Yahweh's voice
and the sound that roars from Yahweh's mouth.
Yahweh flings lightning down
and it strikes anywhere on earth.
After it Yahweh's voice roars again
in the sound of violent thunder.

There is no doubt about it; God shows wonderful things
and performs deeds that we cannot understand.
When God tells the rain to pour down in torrents,
God brings everyone's work to a stop.
Everyone can tell God's work.
Even the wild animals must take shelter from the storm.

Yahweh makes the clouds heavy with water,
and the storm-lightning tears the sky apart.
Yahweh guides the movements of everything.
Whether punishing people
or showing mercy, Yahweh controls the weather and the
    seasons.
Pay attention to all this.

Meditate on God's wonders.
Do you know how God makes lightning?
Do you know how God arranges the clouds?
When you are too hot, can you change the weather?
When you are too cold, can you bring out the sun?
Tell me, what can you say to God?

Yahweh is the mightiest in power.
Yahweh is the most full of justice.
No wonder people respect Yahweh.
No wonder thoughtful people worship Yahweh God with
    reverence.

from The Holy Bible: Job 36 and 37

3 Great Spirit!
  Piler-up of the rocks into towering mountains!
  When you stamp on the stones
  the dust rises and fills the land.
  Hardness of the cliff,
  waters of the pool that turn
  into misty rain when stirred.
  Gourd overflowing with oil!
  Creator . . . who sews the heavens together like cloth,
  knit together everything here on the earth below.
  You are the one who calls the branching trees into life:
  you make new seeds grow out of the ground
  so that they stand straight and strong.
  You have filled the land with people.

  Wonderful one, you live
  among the sheltering rocks.
  You give rain to us people.
  We pray to you,
  hear us, O Strong One!
  When we beg you, show your mercy.
  You are in the highest places
  with the spirits of the great ones.
  You raise the grass-covered hills
  above the earth,
  and you make the rivers.
  Gracious one!   33

  Rozwi, South Africa

4 In the time when God created all things,
  God created the sun;
  and the sun is born and dies and comes again.
  God created the moon;
  and the moon is born and dies and comes again.
  God created the stars;
  and the stars are born and die and come again.
  God created humankind;
  and a human being is born and dies . . . and does not
    come again.   23

  Dinka, Sudan

17

5 Open the windows of heaven,
   give us your blessing!
   Open the windows of heaven,
   give us your blessing!
   Our Maker, [O Nyame], God,
   sweet Creator of us, the church membership.
   Open the windows of heaven,
   give us your blessing!   32

   Fante, Ghana

6 Where I wander – you!
   Where I ponder – you!
   Only you, you again, always you!
   You! You! You!
   When I am gladdened – you!
   When I am saddened – you!
   Only you, you again, always you!
   You! You! You!
   Sky is you, earth is you!
   You above! You below!
   In every trend, at every end,
   Only you, you again, always you!
   You! You! You!   11

   Levi Yitzchak of Berditchev

7 O Lord, O God,
   creator of our land,
   our earth, the trees,
   the animals and humans,
   all is for your honour.
   The drums beat it out,
   and people sing about it,
   and they dance with noisy joy
   that you are the Lord.

   You also have pulled the other continents
   out of the sea.
   What a wonderful world you have made
   out of wet mud,
   and what beautiful men and women!
   We thank you for all the beauty of this earth.

The grace of your creation is like a cool day
between rainy seasons.
We drink in your creation with our eyes.
We listen to the birds' jubilee
with our ears.
How strong and good
and sure your earth smells,
and everything that grows there.

The sky above us
is like a warm, soft Kente cloth,
because you are behind it,
else it would be cold and rough and uncomfortable.
We drink in your creation
and cannot get enough of it.
But in doing this we forget
the evil we have done.

Lord, we call you,
we beg you:
tear us away from our sins
and our death.
This wonderful world fades away.
And one day our eyes snap shut,
and all is over and dead
that is not from you.
We are still slaves of the demons
and the fetishes of this earth,
when we are not saved by you.

Bless us.
Bless our land and people.
Bless our forests with mahogany,
wawa, and cacao.
Bless our fields with cassava and peanuts.
Bless the waters
that flow through our land.
Fill them with fish
and drive great schools of fish to our seacoast,
so that the fishermen in their unsteady boats
do not need to go out too far.
Be with us youth in our countries,

and in all Africa,
and in the whole world.
Prepare us for the service that we should render. 25

Ashanti, Ghana

8 O my Father, Great Elder,
I have no words to thank you,
but with your deep wisdom
I am sure that you can see
how I value your glorious gifts.
O my Father, when I look upon your greatness,
I am overcome with awe.
O Great Elder,
ruler of all things on earth and in heaven,
I am your warrior,
ready to act according to your will. 18

Kikuyu, Kenya

9 My [Nkosi,] Lord, you loved me
before the mountains were strong.
From long ago you anointed me.
I am the beginning of your way.

I am your work of old,
before the large stretches of land were strong;
and the fountains of water
they had not yet spouted strongly.

And the fountains and rivers
before they had flowed strongly
Jehovah created me
before his way.

The depth was not yet there
I was already born,
he had not yet created this heaven
And also this earth.

The sun had not shone yet
in the space of this heaven.
And the moon had not yet shone
In the space of this earth. 10

Zulu, South Africa

10 *This prayer was composed by a first generation Christian. It is included here because of its distinctive African style, and for its evocation of Old Testament prayer forms.*

Thou art the great God, – the one who is in heaven.
It is thou, thou Shield of Truth,
it is thou, thou Tower of Truth,
it is thou, thou Bush of Truth,
it is thou, thou who sittest in the highest,
thou art the creator of life,
thou madest the regions above.
The creator who madest the heavens also,
the maker of the stars and the Pleiades, –
the shooting stars declare it unto us.
The maker of the blind, of thine own will didst thou
    make them.
The trumpet speaks – for us it calls.
Thou art the Hunter who hunts for souls.
Thou art the Leader who goes before us.
Thou art the Great Mantle which covers us.
Thou art he whose hands are wounded;
thou art he whose feet are wounded;
thou art he whose blood is a trickling stream – and why?
Thou art he whose blood was spilled for us.
For this great price we call,
for thine own place we call.   33

Xhosa, South Africa

2

The history of our salvation

Blessed are you, our God from the beginning of things unto the end. And blessed is your name of Glory, which passes all blessings and praise. Yahweh God, you are the only one. You made the heavens with all their beauty, and the earth with everything it bears, and the seas with all they contain.

Yahweh, you are the God who chose Abram, brought him out from the town of Ur and gave him the name Abraham. Because you found him honest, you made a promise and an agreement with him and his descendants. And because you are fair and just, you kept your promise.

You saw the unhappiness of our ancestors in Egypt and you worked wonders against Pharaoh because he treated them badly. You separated the sea in front of them and they passed through without getting wet; but you trapped their wicked enemies in the waters.

During the day you led them with a pillar of cloud, and at night it was a pillar of fire to show them the way. You yourself came down on the mountain called Sinai, and spoke with your people. You gave them rules that are fair and just, and you taught them to know the holy Sabbath day. Through Moses your chosen one, you made laws for your people.

You gave them bread from heaven and water out of the rock. You invited your people to take possession of the land that you had promised to give them. But our ancestors grew

22

proud and disobeyed your commands. They refused to obey, and forgot all the wonderful things you had done for them.

But you are a God of forgiveness, kind and loving, slow to become angry and full of goodness. You did not forget your people, even though they forgot you. Even when they made themselves an idol and worshipped it, you still loved them and did not leave them in the wilderness.

You gave your own Spirit to your people, in order to make them wise. You continued to feed them and to provide drink for them. For forty years in the wilderness, you cared for them; they were lacking nothing, their clothes did not become tattered, and their feet were not swollen.

You gave your people plenty of land. You made the number of their sons increase like the number of the stars in the sky, and you led them into the land that you had promised to their fathers. So your people took possession of that land, with plenty of crops of every kind.

Your chosen people had as much as they could eat, and enjoyed many good things. But they were disobedient to you, and took no notice of your laws. They killed the prophets who warned them about their behaviour, so you punished them by allowing their enemies to catch them.

And when they found life very difficult, your people called out to you for help – and you heard them! And because you still loved them very much, you gave them heroes who set them free. But as soon as they were free, they began to behave badly again, and once more you gave them up to their enemies.

Your people cried out to you again when they were being treated harshly by those enemies, and once more you listened to them. How often do you need to set them free before they learn to live according to your law? They continued to grow proud and to be disobedient, not learning their lesson.

For so many years, you were patient with these people of yours, and kept warning them and giving them chances, even though they would not listen. But, because you loved them so much, you did not abandon them, because you are a loving God. You are our own God, kind and great and mighty.

In everything that has happened to us, you have been full of honour and generosity. When we have shown so much wickedness, you have shown so much kindness and faithfulness. Our ancestors, great and small, did not respect your law, even though you gave them so many good things.

Our ancestors forgot your warnings and took no notice of your commandments, and while they were enjoying their land and all the good things you gave them, they were selfish and greedy, and deaf to you. They did not think of stopping the wickedness they were doing.

And now look at us! We are not free any more. We are here in the land that you provided for our ancestors, that you gave them so that they could enjoy all the good things, but we are not free or happy. For all the wrong things we have done, and for forgetting about you, our God, we are unhappy.

There are still many good things in this land of ours, but all the plentifulness is not being enjoyed by us; other people are making the profit. Because of our sins we are not free. Other people abuse us and our land. We are suffering, Lord. Help us!

from The Holy Bible: Nehemiah 9

OUR WORLD IS WONDERFUL; GOD SAVES IT

Here are two acts of belief, or creeds. They do contain the name of Jesus, unlike most of the other prayers in this book, and they indicate how Jesus came into our world.

12 We believe in God, the Father and Mother; the
        omnipotence of love.
    God is the creator of heaven and earth;
    this whole universe,
    with all its mysteries;
    this earth on which we live,
    and the stars to which we travel.
    God knows us from eternity, God never forgets
    that we are made of the dust of the earth
    and that one day we shall return again to it as dust.

    We believe in Jesus Christ,
    the only beloved Son of God.
    For love of all of us,
    he has willed to share our history, our existence with us.
    We believe that God also wanted to be our God
    in a human way.

God has dwelt as man among us,
a light in the darkness.
But the darkness did not overcome him.
We nailed him to the cross.
And he died and was buried.
But he trusted in God's final word,
and is risen, once and for all;
he said that he would prepare a place for us,
in his Father's house, where he now dwells.

We believe in the Holy Spirit,
who is the Lord and gives life.
And for the prophets among us,
he is language, power and fire.
We believe that together we are all on a journey,
pilgrims, called and gathered together,
to be God's holy people,
for we confess freedom from evil,
the task of bringing justice
and the courage to love.

We believe in eternal life, in love that is stronger than
     death
in a new heaven and a new earth.

Source unknown

3 We believe in the one High God, who out of love created the
beautiful world and everything good in it. He created man
and woman, and wanted them to be happy in the world.
God loves the world and every nation and tribe on the earth.
We have known this High God in the darkness, and now we
know him in the light. God promised in the book of his
word, the bible, that he would save the world and all the
nations and tribes.

   We believe that God made good his promise by sending
his Son, Jesus Christ, a man in the flesh, a Jew by tribe, born
poor in a little village, who left his home and was always on
safari doing good, curing people by the power of God,
teaching about God and humankind, showing that the
meaning of religion is love. He was rejected by his people,
tortured, nailed hands and feet to a cross, and died. He lay
buried in the grave, but the hyaenas did not touch him, and

on the third day he rose from the grave. He ascended to the skies. He is the Lord.

We believe that all our sins are forgiven through him. All who have faith in him must be sorry for their sins, be baptised in the Holy Spirit of God, live the rules of love, and share the bread together in love, to announce the Good News to others until Jesus comes again. We are waiting for him. He is alive. He lives. This we believe.   Amen.   7

Masai, Tanzania

14 And now, Lord, God of Israel, we have sinned, we have been unfaithful; Lord our God, we have broken all your commandments. Let your anger turn from us. Listen, Lord, to our prayers; set us free for the sake of your kindliness and give us your blessings, so that the whole world may know that you are our God.

Look down, Lord, from your holy dwelling-place, and think of us, take notice of us, and listen; look at us Lord, and think again — the person who is overcome with suffering and who goes away bowed down and weak, with failing eyesight and a soul which is hungry, that person is the one to give you glory, Lord, and to do what you ask.

Lord our God, we do not rely only on the merits of our ancestors to offer you our humble request. No, you have sent down your anger on us, as you warned us through the prophets. But we did not listen to your voice, and so you did what you had promised: people died from famine, war and sickness, and it was our own fault. And yet, Lord God, you were good and tender and full of mercy to us.

Almighty God, our troubled heart now cries out to you: Listen, and have pity, Lord, because we have sinned. Hear the prayer of those who sinned and did not listen to your voice: this is why all the disasters have fallen on us. Do not think of the badness of our ancestors, but think of your great power and your great name. You are the Lord our God, and we want to praise you, since you have taught our hearts to respect you, and you encourage us to call on your name. We want to praise you, because we have emptied our hearts of all the evil of those who sin against you. Look on us today, Lord.

from The Holy Bible: Baruch 2 and 3

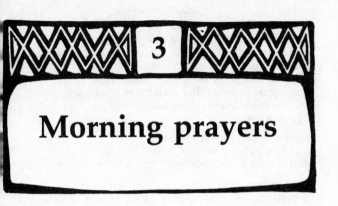

Morning prayers

Lord, my joys mount as do the birds,
heavenwards.
The night has taken wings
and I rejoice in the light.
What a day, Lord! What a day!

Your sun has burned away the dew
from the grass and from our hearts.
What erupts from us,
what encircles us this morning,
is thanksgiving.

Lord, we thank you for all and everything.
Lord, I thank you for what I am,
for my body tall and broad,
despite the meagre meals at school,
and although father has no work.
This body grows and grows
even with malaria in my blood.

Lord, I also thank you
for this job [on the railway],
which I found during my holidays.
I make good money;
the money for school lies already in father's trunk.
You can let me advance far, but I know
I can never outdo your trees.

Lord, I am happy this morning.
Birds and angels sing and I am exultant.
The universe and our hearts are open to your grace.
I feel my body and give thanks.
The sun burns my skin and I thank you.
The breakers are rolling towards the seashore,
the sea foam splashes our house.
I give thanks.

Lord, I rejoice in your creation,
and that you are behind it, and before,
and next to it, and above — and within us.

Lord, your sun is balmy,
it caresses the grass and the cassava out of the clay,
tops it with flowers,
draws out the mahogany,
throws birds into the sky,
and out of us it drums
a song of praise for you.   26 (slightly edited)

Ghana

16   O God, you have prepared in peace the path I must follow
     today. Help me to walk straight on that path. If I speak,
     remove lies from my lips. If I am hungry, take away from me
     all complaint. If I have plenty, destroy pride in me. May I go
     through the day calling on you, you O Lord, who know no
     other Lord.   35

     Galla: Ethiopia

17   Morning of my God, I have been faithful to you all my days.
     God, allow me to proceed through a peaceful life. Grant me,
     God, to continue living in peace as long as you will allow it,
     or even forever. Grant me a life that does not wear out.   29

     Samburu, Kenya

18   [Amma,] God, accept the morning greeting;
     things which come after Amma, accept the morning
        greeting;
     earth, accept the morning greeting;

ancestors, trees, stones, everything,
accept the morning greeting;
you who have placed the stone, accept the morning
you who have balanced the steps, accept the morning
 greeting;
you who slept on beds, accept the morning greeting;
women who bore long-necked calabashes,
accept the morning greeting;
our old men have poured out a libation: take and drink.
If you have drunk, give me a long old age;
make me a gift of children;
let me reach next year.   32

Dogon, Mali

My God, my God, grant me a life that never ends. My God,
my 'kosikosi', grant me what does not end. Grant me what is
desired and goes on forever. My God, grant me what is
searched for and does not end, because always I am like a
little sheep that gives milk, and also I give honey from my
land. 'Shelter-of-the-lambs', hold me tight. My progenitor,
my God, grant me what is desired. Grant me the life of my
children. Watch over me during the night and the day.
Watch over mothers. Grant me what never ends. God, be
watchful, watch over my little ones, both cattle and people;
watch always.   29

Samburu, Kenya

Your works are wonderful – I know it so well.
Who can speak about your might, who can tell your great-
 ness?
Who can record your glory, who can recount your righteous-
 ness?
Who can perceive your signs, who can know your marvels?
Who can comprehend their awe and wonder? Who can
 know your ways?
Lord who can investigate your secrets? Who could penetrate
 your thoughts?
Whose works can equal yours? Who can repay you for your
 goodness?

My God I am ashamed and confused as I stand in your

presence, for I know that compared to your greatness, I am so frail and weak and compared to your perfection, I am so lacking.

For you are one, and you are true life, and you are mighty, and you remain firm, and you are great, and you are wise, and you are God.

And I am just a lump of earth, and a worm; dust from the ground, a cup full of shame, a fleeting shadow, a breeze that goes and does not return.

What am I? What is my life? How strong am I? How righteous am I?

God, I know that the wrongs I have done are too many to be told, and my faults too many to recall.

Nevertheless, I shall recall some of them and confess, though they are like a drop from the ocean.

Perhaps I can calm their uproar and tumult, like the waves and breakers of the sea,

and you will listen and forgive.

I have sinned and I have done wrong. I damaged what was right, and it did not help me.

I turned away from your commands and decisions which were good, but you were just in everything that happened to me because you did rightly, and I acted wickedly.

May it be your will, Lord my God, to crush my evil impulse.

Cover your face so that you do not see my sins and my faults! Do not take me away in the prime of life.

God, I beg you, judge me with mercy and not in anger, lest you annihilate me.

Turn to me in mercy, and bring me back to you in complete repentance, and be with my speech, and with my thoughts, and keep me from sinning with my tongue.

Think of me with love and mercy, and lead me in good ways because of your greatness.

I love you, Lord, for all the goodness which you granted me, and which you will grant me until my dying day.

Strengthen me in the pure love and awe I feel for you.

For all this, I am in duty bound to thank you, and declare the unity of your great name.

For, Lord, there is no God like you, and no deeds like yours.   11

Ibn Gabirol from 'The Crown of Glory'

21 May God protect our elders when they walk and when they
stop, every day ... in the morning that always rises ...
because, my God, we are always blind, my God, we are
always ignorant and do not have eyes to see. My God, we
pray you. My God, we pray you, grant us feet; grant us feet
to walk with. Grant us to taste your fruits; grant me to taste
your fruits. May it be so, my God. There is nothing I know;
for this I have invoked you. Thank you, very much. Grant
me to taste those fruits of yours. Thank you very much, my
God.   29

Samburu, Kenya

22 This, O risen Lord, is the day you have made for us,
a day of happiness and joy!
We pray to you, O Lord:
make each day that you give us,
the most beautiful day of our lives,
because it is the day you have chosen
for us to encounter you, O risen Christ!   5

after Psalm 118

23 O sun, as you rise in the East through God's leadership,
wash away all evils of which I have thought throughout
   the night.
Bless me, so that my enemies will not kill me and my
   family;
guide me through hard work.
O God, give me mercy upon our children who are
   suffering;
bring riches today as the sun rises;
bring all fortunes to me today.   21

Abaluyia, Kenya

24 The Lord rewards me because I do what is right;
God blesses me because I am innocent.
I have obeyed God's law,
I have not turned away from my God.
O Lord God, you are faithful to those who are faithful to
   you;

you save those who are humble,
but you humble those who are proud.
O Lord, you give me light.
You drive away my darkness.

from The Holy Bible: Psalm 18

25 God of truth, you who said to us, 'If today you hear my
voice, do not harden your hearts', we pray to you at the
beginning of this day. You who speak to us through the
marvels of creation, which you give us for our joy: open
our eyes so that we may recognise in your creation the
trace of your steps. You who speak to us through today's
happenings, make us attentive, so as to discern your
holy will in each of our joys and pains. You who speak
to us through our brothers and sisters, help us to
discover your face in the faces of those who surround us.
You who speak to us even in silences: give us the grace
to open our hearts to your calls, to listen to them with
joy, to follow them with love, until the twilight of our
lives, when we will arrive at that eternal today when we
will see you face to face, forever and ever, Amen!

from The Holy Bible: Psalm 95 (adapted)

26 PRAYERS I

Teach us, Lord, the laws of life and the ways of peace.
Yahweh has told you what is good and what the Lord asks
of you. Is it not to do justice, to love mercy, and to walk
humbly with your God!

Micah 6:8

Teach us, Lord, that the more we give, the more we have.
Giving changes a person's impulse to cruelty into kindness of heart. This is the chief service of giving.

Nachman of Bratzlav

Teach us Lord, that in order to change the world, we must
also change ourselves.
The person whom you strengthen for service to God will
love you. The way to strengthen people is to love them.

Nachman of Bratzlav

Teach us, Lord, to accept our limitations.
    It is of great advantage that we shall know our place, and
    not imagine that the whole universe exists for us alone.

Maimonides

Teach us, Lord, to accept our responsibility.
    Every person in Israel should know and consider themself
    as unique in the world . . . and that they are called upon to
    fulfil their particular task.

Chasidic

Teach us, Lord, that within each problem we meet, you have
set an answer.
    There is no stumbling-block one cannot push aside, for
    the stumbling-block is only there for the sake of the will,
    and there actually are no stumbling-blocks save in the
    spirit.

Chas·dic

Teach us, Lord, that love is a giving and not a taking.
    If love depends on some selfish cause, when the cause
    disappears, love disappears; but if love does not depend
    on a selfish cause, it will never disappear.   11

Sayings of the Fathers

27 My heart is ready, God,
    I mean to sing and play,
    I mean to wake the Dawn!
    Yahweh God, I mean to thank you
    and to play music to you;
    your love is as high as heaven;
    let your glory be over the earth!

from The Holy Bible: Psalm 108

28 PRAYERS II

Teach us, Lord, to see more than outward things, and to
trust your voice within us.
    Prefer the truth and right by which you seem to lose, to
    the falsehood and wrong by which you seem to gain.

Maimonides

Teach us, Lord, that we have the right to do the work, but the results are in your hand.
> One may do much or one may do little; it is all one, provided one directs the heart to heaven.

Berachot

Teach us, Lord, that it is not for us to complete the work, but neither may we desist from it.
> Do God's will as if it were your will so that God may do your will as if it were God's will.

Sayings of the Fathers

Teach us, Lord, that this world is not the measure of all things.
> Plan for this world as if you were to live forever; plan for the world to come as if you were to die tomorrow.

Ibn Gabirol

Teach us, Lord, to see in every ending a new beginning.
> The world is like a corridor to the world to come. Prepare yourself in the corridor so that you may enter the inner chamber.

Saying of the Fathers

Teach us, Lord, to consider the mystery of life and death.
> One hour of repentance and good deeds in this world is better than all the life of the world to come; and one hour of calmness of spirit in the world to come is better than all the life of this world. 11

Sayings of the Fathers

29 My God, dawn of my God that rises,
I have preceded you.
Dawn of my God, that comes up from the East
and then goes to fall into the West,
grant us a good life and a lucky one within our hearts.
In fact, we have come before you
so that, my God, you may grant us blessed hearts.
And God said: 'All right'. 29

Samburu, Kenya

Lord our God, and the God of our ancestors, help us to live according to your teaching, and to hold fast to your commands.

God asks us to befriend and honour the old, for we too shall grow old.
> You shall rise in the presence of grey hairs, give honour to the aged, and fear your God. I am the Lord.

Leviticus 19: 32

God asks us to help the poor because our forebears ate the bread of poverty.
> Happy is the one who cares for the poor. The Lord will help that person in a time of need.

Psalm 41: 2

God asks us to welcome the stranger, for we have been homeless many times.
> Share your food with the hungry, bring the homeless into your home.

Isaiah 58: 7

God asks us to rule other creatures as we would have God rule over us.
> It is forbidden to harm any living creature. It is one's duty to save any living creature from pain.

Kitzur Shulchan Aruch

God asks us to protect the weak, for we, too, are weak and pray for God's protection.
> Rob not the poor, nor use the law to crush the weak.

Proverbs 22: 22

God asks us to share the anxieties of others, for God hears them.
> When in my distress I called to the Lord. God's answer was to set me free.

Psalm 118: 5

God commands us to love all people whether they be Jew or non-Jew.
> Love your neighbour as you love yourself. I am the Lord.

Leviticus 19: 18   11

31 O God,
   you gave me peace to pass the night;
   give me peace as well to pass the day.
   Wherever my way may lead,
   which you in peace laid out for me,
   O God, guide my steps.
   In speech, take falsehood away from me,
   in hunger take murmuring from me,
   in fulness take complacency from me.
   I pass the day invoking you,
   O lordless Lord.   4

   Galla, Ethiopa

32 PRAYERS IV

   Lord our God, and the God of our ancestors, help us to live
   according to your teaching and to hold fast to your commands.

   God asks us to overcome our prejudice, for we have been,
   and are, the victim of prejudice.
      Are not you and the Ethiopians all the same to me,
      children of Israel? — It is the Lord who speaks.

   Amos 9: 7

   God asks us to visit the sick, for our bodies too are frail.
      We should pay attention to the needs of the sick, to care
      for them, give them pleasure and pray for mercy for them.

   Kitzur Shulchan Aruch

   God asks us to transform enmity, for are we not our own
   enemies?
      Who is mighty among the mighty? The person who
      controls passion and makes a friend out of an enemy.

   Avot d'Rabbi Natan

   God asks us to support the disabled, for some are disabled
   in body and some in spirit.
      You shall not treat the deaf with contempt, nor make the
      blind stumble.

   Leviticus 19: 14

   God asks us to understand those who are sick in mind, for
   who among us knows all reality?

Hold no one insignificant and nothing improbable, for everyone has their hour, and everything has its place.

Sayings of the Fathers

God asks us to seek out the lonely, for this is the meaning of community.
You stand this day all of you before the Lord, all of you are pledges one for the other.

Tanchuma

God asks us to strengthen ourselves, for the task God has given us needs all the strength we possess.
Love the Lord your God with all your heart and all your soul and all your might. 11

Deuteronomy 6: 5

33 I am God's creature and my fellow is God's creature.
My work is in the town and his/her work is in the country.
I rise early for my work and (s)he rises early for his/her work.
Just as (s)he does not presume to do my work, so I do not presume to do his/her work.
Will you say, I do much and (s)he does little?
We have learnt: One may do much or one may do little; it is all one, provided one directs one's heart to heaven.

Berachot 11

34 PRAYERS V

You are the Lord of creation and the guardian of Israel. Your truth has been our strength and your righteousness our purpose in every generation.

We are your vineyard and you are our keeper.
As the vine will receive no graft from another tree, so the community of Israel accepts no ruler but God.

Zohar

We are your work and you are our creator.
Everyone who acts in justice and truth is a partner with God in the work of creation.

Mechilta

We are your beloved and you are our friend.
I have loved you with an everlasting love, and so I stretch
my faithful care upon you.

Jeremiah 31: 3

We are your very own and you are our nearest.
The Lord has declared today that you are God's own
people, as was promised you, but only if you keep all the
commands of God.

Deuteronomy 26: 18

We are your people and you are our ruler.
Accept the yoke of the realm of heaven, and practise love
and kindness to one another.

Sifre

We are your acknowledged people and you are our acknowledged God.
It is our duty to praise the Lord of all, to recognise the
greatness of the creator of first things.   11

Aleynu Prayer

35 In the beginning was God,
today is God,
tomorrow will be God.
Who can make an image of God?
God has no body.
God is a word which comes out of your mouth.
That word! It is no more, it is past, and still it lives!
So is God.   21

Pygmy, Zaire

36 May the God of peace be with me;
may God help me;
may God give me peace.
In the name of God, my hand,
my creator, my hand.
May God give me the blessing of the weaver.
From the morning to the evening may I remain seated.
Who is the creator of the woven thread?
It is I, I am the creator of the weaver's thread.   6

Peul/Fulani, West Africa

37 Sing to God, all the world,
   worship God with joy.
   Come into God's presence
   with happy songs.

   Admit that God is truly our God.
   God made us: we are God's own children,
   God's people and God's flock.

   Go into the gates of the Temple
   with thanksgiving.
   Give thanks and praise to God.
   God is very good.
   God's love lasts forever.
   God's faithfulness will never end.

   from The Holy Bible: Psalm 100

38 Our Father in heaven,
   may your name be held holy,
   your kingdom come
   your will be done,
   on earth as in heaven.
   Give us today our daily bread.
   And forgive us our debts
   as we have forgiven those who are in debt to us.
   And do not put us to the test
   but save us from the evil one.

   The Holy Bible: Matthew 6: 9-13 (Jerusalem Bible)

39 May God agree with us.
   Yes, my God, you will save us;
   yes, my God, you will guide us,
   and your thoughts will be with us night and day.
   Grant us to remain a long time
   like the great wing of rain, like the long rains.
   Give us the fragrance of a purifying branch.
   Be the support of our burdens,
   and may they always be untied,
   the shells of fertility and mothers and children.
   God be our safeguard, also where the shepherds are.
   God, sky, with stars at your sides

and the moon in the middle of your stomach,
morning of my God that is rising,
come and hit us with your blessed wind:
flood us with your waters.
And God said: 'All right'.   29

Samburu, Kenya

40 PRAYERS VI

Blessed are you, Lord our God, ruler of the universe, who
takes away sleep from my eyes and slumber from my
eyelids.

The Lord is my shepherd
I shall not want.
In green fields God lets me lie
by quiet streams God leads me.
Surely goodness and mercy will be with me
all the days of my life,
and I shall live in the house of the Lord forever.

May I always remember God when I am alone and when I
am with others; speak the truth and keep the truth in my
heart.

HEAR O ISRAEL, THE LORD IS OUR GOD, THE LORD IS
ONE. LOVE THE LORD YOUR GOD WITH ALL YOUR
HEART, AND ALL YOUR SOUL, AND ALL YOUR MIGHT.

My God, keep my tongue from causing harm and my lips
from telling lies. Open my heart to your teachings and help
me to do them.

May the words I speak aloud and the thoughts that lie
within my heart always please you, Lord, who gives me
strength and saves me.

The wolf shall live with the lamb,
the leopard lie down with the kid,
the calf and the young lion shall feed together,
and a little child shall lead them.
They shall not hurt nor destroy
in all my holy mountain.   11

41 Yahweh God, let my prayers reach your ears, and pay a little
    attention to my sad cries. Listen to me when I shout for help,
    because you are my Creator and my God.

    I am saying this prayer to you, God, for in the morning you
    listen to my voice, and at dawn I am ready and waiting for
    you; I am on the watch for you.

    You, O God, are not pleased with wickedness, and you have
    no sympathy for those who are deliberately bad. Those who
    boast and show off their good fortune, collapse in your
    sight.

    But because your love is so great, I know that I can come
    before you, and as I stand in your presence I can bow down
    before you and offer respect and reverence to you.

    Yahweh God, lead me in the ways of your justice, because
    there are people who lie in wait to trap me. So I am begging
    you to make your ways very clear to me.

    Not a word that comes from the mouths of evil people can be
    trusted; deep within them there is ruin. Their throats are
    wide open like graves, and yet they pretend to speak with
    such sweetness and truth.

    There is joy for everyone who takes shelter in you, and that
    joy is without end. Because you protect them, they are
    happy to be with you, and they love your name.

    Lord God, you are always showering your blessings on
    those who try to be good, and your kindness and concern
    are like a shield or a blanket to cover them.

    from The Holy Bible: Psalm 5

42 Morning has risen;
    [Asobe,] God, take away from us every pain,
    every ill,
    every mishap;
    Asobe, let us come safely home.   23
    Pygmy, Zaire

4

Praise
Thanksgiving

43 Thank you very, very much;
my God, thank you.
Give me food today,
food for my sustenance every day.
Thank you very, very much.   29

Samburu, Kenya

44 O my Father, Great Elder,
I have no words to thank you,
but with your deep wisdom
I am sure that you can see
how I value your glorious gifts.
O my Father, when I look upon your greatness,
I am confounded with awe.
O Great Elder,
Ruler of all things earthly and heavenly,
I am your warrior,
ready to act in accordance with your will.   18

Kikuyu, Kenya

45 The year has come round, O great [Odomankoma,] God,
never can we thank you for your deeds and blessing for
us.

Come now and eat from our hands and bless your
    people.
Let all who are ill get well.
Let all who are barren bear children.
Let all who are impotent find remedy.
Do not let them go blind or paralysed.
We beseech happiness, let us have it.

Ashanti, Ghana

46 I will give thanks to you, Yahweh,
      and praise you, God my saviour;
      I give thanks to your name,
      for you have been a protector and support to me,
      and redeemed my body from destruction,
      from the traps of those who tell lies against me,
      from lips that fabricate falsehood;

      and in the presence of those around me
      you have supported me and set me free,
      true to the greatness of your mercy and of your name,
      from the sharp teeth of those who want to make a meal
        of me,
      from the hands of those who want my life,
      from the many difficulties I have suffered,
      from the stifling heat which oppressed me,
      from the heart of a fire that I had not lit,

      from the deep belly of the underworld,
      from the contaminated tongue and the lying word —
      from the lying tongue slandering me before the King.
      I have been close to death,
      my life had gone down to the very brink of the
        underworld.
      Enemies were surrounding me on every side,
      there was no one to support me;
      I looked unsuccessfully for someone to help me.

      Then I remembered your mercy, O God,
      and your deeds from earliest times,
      and how you set free those who wait patiently for you,
      and how you save them from the clutches of their
        enemies.
      And from earth I sent up my request for help,
      I begged to be delivered from death,

I called on you, God, to save me,
do not desert me on the day of my ordeal,
in the time of my helplessness against the proud.

I will praise your name without ceasing,
and gratefully sing its praises.
And my request for help was heard,
for you saved me from destruction,
you delivered me from that time of evil.
And therefore I will thank and praise you,
and bless the name of the Lord.

from The Holy Bible: Ecclesiasticus 51: 1-14

47 Yahweh God, I turn towards you, and pray for those I love,
who are dearer to me than life. Protect them as a parent, and
keep them from harm, in body, mind and spirit. Deepen
their desire to know your will, and strengthen them to do it.
Help them in their struggle with the world, with selfishness,
with laziness, and with forgetfulness of their own souls.
Help me as well, so that my own life does not contradict the
life I desire for them. Let it serve them as an example, and
help them in their struggle for goodness.

I thank you for those who are dear to me, for the privilege
of guiding their steps towards you, for the love which binds
our hearts together, for its joy, for its solace, and for the
strength it gives me in trouble and temptation. Help me to
keep that love strong. May no selfishness or misunder-
standing weaken it. May it bless me to the end! Amen. 11

48 Even on this day of rest, I think of the working days which
lie ahead, and ask for your blessing on them. You are with
me in the peace and holiness of the Sabbath day, be with me
even more in the stress and strain of the world. Therefore I
ask you above all to bless my daily work. Let me do it for its
own sake, and not for my own advantage; and let it show my
service, not my selfishness. In this way I shall be at peace
with my soul, and closer in sympathy and friendship to my
fellow men and women. Keep me from laziness, and help
me to perfect myself, so that the world in which I live comes
nearer to its perfection. Help me to measure all things by the
standard of goodness and not by the standard of wordly

success. Let humble work be honourable for me. Let me prefer it to works whose fruits are vanity and strife. Help me to realise that there is a goal beyond my livelihood, and that there is a purpose on earth greater than comfort. Let this knowledge save me from undue sadness and despair when I have my share of failure. I cast on you my burden of anxiety and fear, for you know what is best for me. In riches and poverty, success and failure, you are with me, and in them all I learn to see your face. Amen.   11

49 Wisdom is the finest beauty of a person.
    Money does not prevent you from becoming blind.
    Money does not prevent you from becoming mad,
    money does not prevent you from becoming lame.
    You may be ill in any part of your body, so it is better
       for you to go and think again
    and to select wisdom.
    Come and sacrifice, that you may have rest in your body,
    inside and outside.

    African

50 *The prayer of a shepherd who 'did not know how to pray':*

    Lord of the Universe! It is apparent and known unto you,
    that if you had cattle and gave them to me to tend, though I
    take wages for tending from all others, from you I would
    take nothing, because I love you.   11

    Sefer Chasidim

51 Yahweh, you are my God,
    I extol you, I praise your name;
    for you have carried out your excellent design,
    long planned, trustworthy, true.
    For you have made the town a heap of stones,
    the fortified city a ruin.
    The citadel of the proud is a city no longer,
    it will never be rebuilt.
    Hence a mighty people gives you glory,
    the city of pitiless nations holds you in awe;
    for you are a refuge for the poor,

a refuge for the needy in distress,
a shelter from the storm,
a shade from the heat;
while the breath of pitiless men
is like the winter storm.
Like drought in a dry land
you will repress the clamour of the proud;
like heat by the shadow of a cloud
the singing of the despots will be subdued.

The Holy Bible: Isaiah 25: 1-5 (Jerusalem Bible)

52 Great is, O King,
   our happiness
   in thy kingdom,
   thou, our king.

   We dance before thee,
   our king,
   by the strength
   of thy kingdom.

   May our feet
   be made strong;
   let us dance before thee,
   eternal.

   Give ye praise,
   all angels,
   to him above
   who is worthy of praise.   34

   Zulu, South Africa

53 THE SONG OF THE THREE YOUNG MEN IN THE FIRE

   'May you be blessed, God of our ancestors,
   be praised and spoken of forever.
   Blessed be your glorious and holy name,
   be praised and spoken of forever.
   May you be blessed in the Temple of your sacred glory,
   be exalted and glorified forever.
   Blessed, you searcher of great depths, seated on angels,
   be exalted and glorified forever;
   blessed are you in heaven,
   be exalted and glorified forever.

'All things the Lord has made, bless the Lord:
give God glory and eternal praise.
Angels of the Lord! all bless the Lord:
give God glory and eternal praise.
Heavens! bless the Lord:
give God glory and eternal praise.
Waters above the heavens! bless the Lord:
give God glory and eternal praise.
Powers of the Lord! all bless the Lord:
give God glory and eternal praise.
Sun and moon! bless the Lord:
give God glory and eternal praise.
Stars of heaven! bless the Lord:
give God glory and eternal praise.
Showers and dews! all bless the Lord:
give God glory and eternal praise.
Winds! all bless the Lord:
give God glory and eternal praise.
Fire and heat! bless the Lord:
give God glory and eternal praise.
Cold and heat! bless the Lord:
give God glory and eternal praise.
Dews and sleet! bless the Lord:
give God glory and eternal praise.
Frost and cold! bless the Lord:
give God glory and eternal praise.
Ice and snow! bless the Lord:
give God glory and eternal praise.
Nights and days! bless the Lord:
give God glory and eternal praise.
Light and darkness! bless the Lord:
give God glory and eternal praise.
Lightning and clouds! bless the Lord:
give God glory and eternal praise.
Let the earth bless the Lord,
give God glory and eternal praise.
Mountains and hills! bless the Lord:
give God glory and eternal praise.
Every thing that grows on the earth! bless the Lord:
give God glory and eternal praise.
Springs of water! bless the Lord:
give God glory and eternal praise.
Seas and rivers! bless the Lord:

give God glory and eternal praise.
Sea beasts and everything that lives in water! bless the
    Lord:
give God glory and eternal praise.
Birds of heaven! all bless the Lord:
give God glory and eternal praise.
Animals wild and tame! all bless the Lord:
give God glory and eternal praise.
Sons and daughters! bless the Lord:
give God glory and eternal praise.
Israel! bless the Lord:
give God glory and eternal praise.
Priests! bless the Lord:
give God glory and eternal praise.
Servants of the Lord! bless the Lord:
give God glory and eternal praise.
Spirits and souls of the virtuous! bless the Lord:
give God glory and eternal praise.
Devout and humble-hearted people! bless the Lord:
give God glory and eternal praise.
Ananiah, Azariah, Mishael! bless the Lord:
give God glory and eternal praise.
For God has snatched us from the underworld,
saved us from the hand of death,
saved us from the burning fiery furnace,
rescued us from the heart of the flame.
Give thanks to the Lord, for God is good,
for God's love is everlasting.
All you who worship, bless the God of gods,
praise and give thanks,
for God's love is everlasting.'

The Holy Bible, Daniel 3: 52-90 (Jerusalem Bible, adapted)

54 THANKSGIVING AFTER MEALS

We have eaten and been satisfied. May we not be blind to
the needs of others, nor deaf to their cry for food. Open our
eyes and our hearts so that we may share your gifts, and help
to remove hunger and want from our world.

The Lord gives strength to his people, the Lord blesses his
people with peace.

May what we have eaten satisfy us, what we have drunk refresh us, and what we have left be for a blessing. For it is written: 'So he set it before them, and they ate and some was left over, as the Lord had said' (*2 Kings 4: 44*).

You are blessed by the Lord, maker of heaven and earth.

Blessed is the man who trusts in the Lord and puts his confidence in him.

The Lord gives strength to his people. The Lord blesses his people with peace.

> Rock by whose gift we eat,
> bless him, my faithful ones,
> for we have been satisfied
> and food is left over,
>   as was the word of the Lord.

He feeds all his world,
our shepherd, our father.
We have eaten his bread,
we have drunk of his wine,
now therefore we thank him
and praise with our mouths;
we say and we sing
    none is holy as the Lord.

> Rock by whose gift we eat,
> bless him, my faithful ones,
> for we have been satisfied
> and food is left over,
>   as was the word of the Lord.

With song and thanksgiving
let us now bless our God
for the plentiful land
which our fathers received.
He has given us food
for our bodies and souls.
His mercy protects us,
    ever true is the Lord.

> Rock by whose gift we eat,
> bless him, my faithful ones,
> for we have been satisfied
> and food is left over,
>   as was the word of the Lord.   11

Jewish Thanksgivings after Meals

55 Praise rightfully belongs to you,
    God,
    vows made to you must be kept,
    because you answer prayer.

All human beings must come to you
with all their sins;
although our faults overwhelm us,
you cover them over.

The ones you choose are happy,
you invite them to live with you.
Fill us with the good things
of your holy Temple.

Your generosity and justice
overwhelm us with happiness,
God our saviour,
hope of all people on earth and the distant islands.

Your strength holds up the mountains,
so great is your power.
You calm the stormy ocean,
the noise of its waves.

The people of the earth are in turmoil and panic,
wherever they live in the world,
but the wonders you do bring shouts of joy
to the gateways of morning and evening.

You visit the earth and water it,
you weigh it down with riches;
God's rivers overflow with water
to provide good crops for the earth.

This is how you provide earth's harvest,
by drenching the land and levelling the farms,
by softening it with showers, by blessing the first-fruits.
You bring the year to a happy end with your goodness.

Wherever you pass, abundance is to be found;
the desert produces rich lands,
the hillsides are wrapped in joy,
the fields are dressed with sheep and goats,
the valleys are clothed in grain.
What shouts of joy! What singing!

from The Holy Bible: Psalm 66

56 We praise the living God and him do we adore
who is outside the bounds of space and time.

Unique is he, and none like him can ever be
beyond all limitations men define.

He has no human form, no likeness to a man;
more wonderful than any holiness we know.

Before he had begun creation of our world,
he was the first, with no beginning of his own.

Behold he is the Lord of all the universe
who teaches every creature; he is king.

And to the world he speaks, and freely gives his word
through prophets that he chooses to proclaim his will.

Another man like Moses, Israel has not known,
a prophet who to God could be so close.

God gave his people truth by which to lead their life
taught by the faithful prophet of his house.

God will never change the teaching that he gave
and he will put no other in its place.

He watches and he knows the secrets in our hearts,
before each deed, its ending he can trace.

The man of loving deeds rejoices in his love,
but evil leads to evil which destroys.

And at the end of days, an anointed he will send
redeeming those who wait for when he saves.

Life beyond all death, he gives through his great love.
We bless for evermore his glorious name.   11

from the Sabbath Evening Service
(Reform Synagogues of GB)

57 Lord our God, be pleased with your people Israel and listen
to their prayers. In your great mercy delight in us so that
your presence may rest upon Zion. Our eyes look forward to
your return to Zion in mercy! Blessed are you Lord, who
restores your presence to Zion.

We declare with gratitude that you are our God and the
God of our ancestors forever. You are our rock, the rock of

our life and the shield that saves us. In every generation we thank you and recount your praise for our lives held in your hand, for our souls that are in your care, and for the signs of your presence that are with us every day. At every moment, at evening, morning and noon, we experience your wonders and your goodness. You are goodness itself, for your mercy has no end. You are mercy itself, for your love has no limit. Forever have we put our hope in you.   11

from the Daily Amidah (Reform Synagogues of GB)

58 PRAYER OF KING DAVID

Lord Yahweh, there is none like you, no God but you alone, as our own ears have heard. Is there another people on earth like your people Israel, with a God setting out to redeem them and make them God's own people, make them famous, work great and terrible things on their behalf, drive nations out, and other gods too? You have made us your own people forever; and you, Yahweh, have become our God. Now, Lord, always keep the promise you have made me, your servant, and my family.

Do as you have said. Your name will be held in respect for ever, and people will say: 'Yahweh God is God over Israel'. The family of your servant David will be made secure in your presence, since you yourself, God, have made this revelation to me. It is for this reason that I have been moved to offer this prayer to you. Yes, Lord Yahweh, you are God indeed, your words are true and you have made this fair promise to your servant. Be pleased, then, to bless my family, so that it may continue forever in your presence; for you, Lord Yahweh, have spoken; and with your blessing my family will indeed be blessed forever.

from The Holy Bible: 2 Samuel 7: 22-29

59 THE SONG OF HANNAH
(compare Mary's response to the Angel in Luke 1: 46-55)

My heart exults in Yahweh,
my spirit rejoices in my God,
my mouth dismisses those who are against me,
for I rejoice in your saving power.

There is none as holy as Yahweh,
(indeed there is none but you),
no rock like our God.
Do not keep on speaking with proud words,
do not let arrogance come from your mouth.
For Yahweh is an all-knowing God,
who takes account of our deeds.
The bow of the strong man is broken,
but the weak have dressed themselves in strength.
The overfed hire themselves, to get still more food,
but the hungry stop working.
The barren woman produces seven children,
but the mother of many children becomes unhappy.
Yahweh gives death and life;
Yahweh makes poor and rich,
Yahweh humbles and also exalts.
Yahweh raises the poor from the dust,
and lifts the needy from the rubbish dump
to give them a place next to the rich,
and to offer them a seat of honour;
for to Yahweh the earth's supports belong,
on these Yahweh has balanced the world.
Yahweh keeps the steps of faithful people safe,
but the wicked vanish in darkness
(because it is not by strength that people triumph).
The enemies of Yahweh God are shattered,
the Most High thunders in the heavens.
Yahweh judges the whole earth from end to end,
and gives God's own power to the chosen one,
Yahweh exalts the spirit of the anointed one.

from The Holy Bible: 1 Samuel 2: 1-10

60   *This is a prayer from a fisherman of Ghana; it is influenced by Christian
ideas and language*

Lord, I sing your praise
the whole day through, until the night.
Dad's nets are filled; I have helped him.
We have drawn them in, stamping the rhythm with our
    feet,
the muscles tense.
We have sung your praise.

On the beach there were our mammies,
who bought the blessings out of the nets,
out of the nets and into their basins.
They rushed to the market, returned and bought again.
Lord, what a blessing is the sea, with fish in plenty.
Lord, that is the story of your grace:
nets tear, and we succumb because we cannot hold them.
Lord, with your praise we drop off to sleep.
Carry us through the night.
Make us fresh for the morning.
Halleluiah for the day!
And blessing for the night!   Amen.   26

Ghana

61 God, I thank you for this time of prayer, when I become
conscious of your presence, and lay before you my desires,
my hopes and my gratitude. This consciousness, this inner
certainty of your presence is my greatest blessing. My life
would be empty if I did not have it, if I lost you in the maze
of the world, and if I did not return to you from time to time,
to be at one with you, certain of your existence and your
love. It is good that you are with me in all my difficulties and
troubles, and that I have in you a friend whose help is sure
and whose love never changes.

   I thank you also for the light and truth which shine out
from your word; for the holy words written down by those
whose souls were touched by your spirit; for the teaching
and the call which reach me from your messengers, which
come from their very lips. Help me to transform my thanks
into service. Let my mind and my soul add to the holiness of
life. May all that I have learnt in my worship here stay with
me and keep me in goodness, so that my actions may be
pure and my soul be at peace in the dust and heat of the
world. Amen.   11

Jewish prayer

62 Almighty God, I praise you, and bless you for the week that
has passed, for your protection and your mercy which have
brought me safely through its difficulties and dangers. I
thank you for the joys which have lightened it, for the
strength which has upheld me in the worldly fight, and for

the joy and rapture of the struggle itself. If the swift passing of the days has dulled their true meaning, if I have failed to hear your voice in the clamour of the world and recognise your presence in its blinding glare, please forgive me. I will try to do better in the days to come. You are my creator, and what can I do alone? What is my strength – without your aid!

Help me then, I beg you. Strengthen and bless the goodness in me. Help me to see more clearly what is worthwhile, and to keep it more faithfully. Help me to pursue the true ideals I know with more purpose and determination. Then when this holy day of rest comes round again, it may mark another step on my way through life, on my way to the perfect peace that dwells forever with you. Amen.   11

Jewish prayer

63 Who is like you, revealing the deeps,
       fearful in praises, doing wonders?

The creator who discovers all from nothing
is revealed to the heart, but not to the eye;
therefore ask not how nor where –
       for God fills heaven and earth.

Remove lust from the midst of you;
you will find your God within you,
walking gently in your heart.
       The one who brings low and lifts up.

And see the way of the soul's secret,
search it out and refresh yourself.
God will make you wise, and you will find freedom,
       for you are a captive and the world is a prison.

Make knowledge the envoy between yourself and God.
Annul your will and do God's will,
and know that wherever you hide, God's eye is there,
       and nothing is too hard for God.

God was the Living One, while there was yet no dust of
       the world,
and God is the maker and the bearer,
and a human being is counted as a fading flower –
       soon to fade, as fades a leaf.   11

Judah Halevi

55

5

Food and crops
Planting and
harvesting

64 Whoever is not prosperous
   may that one enjoy immeasurable prosperity.
   Those who are fishermen among us,
   if they go out with their nets
   may their nets bring them prosperity.
   If anyone should wish evil to follow the nets
   may this evil come upon the one who plans this evil.
   May we enjoy good health
   so that we may all continue to serve you.
   Women, men, and relations of every degree
   may they all be safe and sound.
   May we never suffer any evil.
   May peace abound forever.
   May it come to rain
   so that our crops may produce abundantly,
   and when we sell them
   they must earn plenty of money
   to fill our rooms
   so that we can continue to serve you.   12

   Anlo Ewe, Ghana

65 May our yams,
   which we are going to plant in the earth this year,
   be good.
   May children be born.

May we have enough to eat.
Let us live.
If anyone should cast a spell over anyone else,
let that one die.
Let peace reign among us.   6

Yakö, Nigeria

The Lord is my shepherd;
there is nothing I shall want.
Fresh and green are the pastures
where he gives me repose.

Near restful waters he leads me,
to revive my drooping spirit.
He guides me along the right path;
he is true to his name.

If I should walk in the valley of darkness
no evil would I fear.
You are there with your crook and your staff;
with these you give me comfort.

You have prepared a banquet for me
in the sight of my foes.
My head you have anointed with oil;
my cup is overflowing.

Surely goodness and kindness shall follow me
all the days of my life.
In the Lord's own house shall I dwell
forever and ever.

The Holy Bible: Psalm 23 (Jerusalem Bible)

The edges of the years have met,
I take sheep and new yams
and give that you may eat.
Life to me.
Life to this my Ashanti people.
Women who cultivate the farms, when they do so,
grant that the food comes forth in abundance.
Do not allow any illnesses to come.   21

Ashanti, Ghana

68 O God, you have formed heaven and earth;
   you have given me all the goods that the earth bears!
   Here is your part, my God.
   Take it!   24

   Pygmy, Zaire

69 Yes! Yes! I implore you, O grandfathers who completed so
   many noble undertakings! Having sacrificed this bull
   which belongs to you, I pray to you, asking of you every
   kind of prosperity. I cannot deny you nourishment, since
   you have given me all the herds that are here, and if you ask
   me the nourishment that you have given me, is it not just
   that I return it to you? Grant us many beasts to fill these
   tables! Grant us much grain, so that many people may come
   to inhabit this village which is yours and so may make much
   tumult to your glory. Grant us numerous offspring, so that
   this village may be much populated and your names may
   never be extinguished!   23

   Zulu, South Africa

70 O [Nyambe,] God, you are the creator of all. Today we your
   creatures prostrate ourselves before you in supplication. We
   have no strength. You who have created us have all power.
   We bring you our seed and all our implements, that you may
   bless them and bless us also, so that we may make good use
   of them by the power which comes from you, our creator.

   Lozi, Zambia   23

71 Hail, hail, hail.
   May happiness come.
   May meat come.
   May corn come.
   Just as the farmers work
   and look forward to the reaping,
   so may we sit again as we are sitting now.
   May our enemies turn from us and go . . .
   Lord, return.   32

   Ga, Ghana

58

2 The time of harvest is over;
   you have given us good crops;
   we are going into the bush.
   Now I call on you,
   so that no evil falls on us
   and our feet do not step on anything bad,
   and that we meet nothing but good things
   and that nothing bad touches us:
   you guaranteed these things
   and have kept your promise.
   May the animals in the bush come to meet us;
   let them come within our circle.
   Let our arrows not miss them;
   let our arrows kill them.
   Let the arrows not kill any of us.
   You who have given such a good harvest
   continue to walk before us
   as you have been doing for our grandparents.   6

Betammaribé (Somba), Dahomey (Benin)

3 O God, show kindness and bless us
   and let your face shine its light on us.
   For then the earth will acknowledge your ways
   and all the nations will know of your power to save.
   Let the peoples praise you, O God;
   let all the peoples praise you.

   Let the nations be glad and sing for joy,
   since you rule the world with justice.
   With fairness you rule the peoples,
   you guide the nations on earth.
   Let the peoples praise you, O God;
   let all the peoples praise you.

   The soil has given its harvest,
   God, our God, has blessed us.
   May God still give us his blessing
   till the ends of the earth show him respect.
   Let the peoples praise you, O God;
   let all the peoples praise you.

from The Holy Bible: Psalm 67

Faith Trust
Peace

74 The wicked man does not know the word of God but only hears the voice of sin. He does not respect and fear God. He flatters himself so much that he cannot see and be ashamed of his guilt. Everything he says is wicked and deceitful; he has turned his back on wisdom.

Even when he is in bed, the wicked man is plotting how to do more wickedness. He continues with his evil ways and never keeps away from what is bad.

Yahweh God, your love reaches to the heavens and your faithfulness reaches as high as the clouds. Your justice is like a tall mountain, and your judgement is as deep as the ocean's depths.

Yahweh, you are the protector of men and women, and animals too; how precious is the love you have for us! It is for this reason that we take shelter in your shadow. People can feast on the plenty of your house, and you give them drink from your river of pleasure. With you, God, is the fountain of life.

By your light we see the light. Do not stop loving those who know you, and do not stop being good to honest people. Do not let the feet of proud men crush me, or wicked hands abuse me. The evil men have fallen down – there they lie, beaten down to the ground. They will never stand again.

from The Holy Bible: Psalm 36

5 For your blessing we thank you, God: faith in you.
Increase it, we beg, so that we no longer doubt.
Drive out all our miserliness, so that we do not refuse you
  anything.
Increase our faith, for the sake of those without faith.
Make us instruments of your faith, for those with only a
  little.
Fill our bodies with faith, our bodies that work for you all
  our days.
Help us to avoid the enemies of our faith, or to overcome
  them.
You are with us in confrontations; this we believe.
In your hands we place ourselves, and are secure.
Make haste to enter our hearts; make haste.   27

Masai, Tanzania

6 Yahweh God, more and more people are turning away from
me, more and more are rebelling against me, more and more
are saying about me: 'That one will get no help from God'.
But Yahweh God, the shield which encircles me, you are my
glory and you can help me to hold up my head.

  I cry out in a loud voice to Yahweh my God, and Yahweh
answers me from the holy mountain. Now I can lie down
and go to sleep and then awake, because Yahweh has hold of
me. There is no need to fear those tens of thousands posted
against me wherever I turn.

  Rise up, Yahweh! Save me, my God! You injure my
enemies on their cheekbones, and you break the teeth of
those who are wicked.

  From Yahweh God comes rescue.

  On your people, God, let your blessing fall!

from The Holy Bible: Psalm 3

7 You know, dear God, that my people still believe much in
juju. But I don't believe in it anymore, since I believe in you.
But sometimes I am afraid of it. Now they are trying again to
get at me with juju. They want to put something bad in my
head. They believe in it.

  They drum for it, they dance for it, and they sing for it.
And I can do nothing about it. I don't believe in it any more,
but I am still afraid of it. You are much stronger than juju.

Halleluja! Halleluja! You are my God, mine, mine, mine.

My great God, great, great, great. My strong God, strong, strong, strong. My loving God, loving, loving, loving. My redeemer, my saviour. My hut, my shadow, my redeemer, my redeemer, redeemer.

You are my cave, my door, my weapon, when evil ones are making juju against me. But you are still stronger, much, much stronger. They are dancing around the drums. They are making juju against me. But I will depend entirely on you. I can do nothing against this juju.

I won't get another fetish-priest. I'll depend entirely on you. Even when I am sick I won't get a fetish-priest. Yes, I have you. You are always there. I depend on you. I thank, thank, thank you. What is juju against you? Juju can do nothing where you are. Amen.   25

Ghana

78 You, Father, who do not die,
    you who do not know death
    and whose life is always so animated
    without knowing the cold of sleep [death],
    all your children have come here.

    They have all gathered round you.
    Surround them with your power, O Father.
    May your shade penetrate into them,
    you, Father, who do not die,
    you, Father of our people [race].   6

Fan, Cameroon-Congo

79 How much longer will you forget me, Yahweh God? For
        ever?
    How much longer will you hide your face from me?
    How much longer must I endure grief in my soul,
    and sorrow in my heart by day and by night?
    How much longer must my enemy succeed against me?
    Look, and answer me, Yahweh my God!

    Give my eyes light, or I shall sleep in death,
    and my enemy will say: 'I have beaten that one',
    and my oppressors have the joy of seeing me stumble.
    But I for my part rely on your love, Yahweh;

let my heart rejoice in your saving help.
Let me sing to Yahweh for the goodness God has shown
me.

The Holy Bible, Psalm 13 (Jerusalem Bible, adapted)

30 May accidents stay far away from us. Leave freshness in the
village. Let everyone live. May everything be fresh and cool
and peaceful. May accidents stay far away. May the people
do the farmwork in peace. Let no fire burn us.   6

Yakö, Nigeria

31 *Tobit, blinded, puts himself trustfully in God's hands; later, his sight is
restored.*

You are just, O Lord, and all your works are just.
All your ways are grace and truth, and you are the Judge
of the world.

Therefore, Lord, remember me, look on me.
Do not punish me for my sins
or for my heedless faults
or for those of my fathers.

For we have sinned against you
and broken your commandments;
and you have given us over to be plundered, to captivity
and death,
to be the talk, the laughing-stock and scorn of all the
nations
among whom you have dispersed us.

Whereas all your decrees are true
when you deal with me as my faults deserve,
and those of my fathers,
since we have neither kept your commandments,
nor walked in truth before you;
so now, do with me as you will; be pleased to take my
life from me;
I desire to be delivered from earth and to become earth
again.
For death is better to me than life.

I have been criticised and abused without cause,
and I am distressed without measure.

Lord, I wait for the sentence you will give
to deliver me from this affliction.
Let me go away to my everlasting home;
do not turn your face from me, O Lord.
For it is better to die than still to live in the face of
  trouble
that knows no pity; I am weary of hearing myself
  betrayed.

from The Holy Bible, Tobit 3: 2-6

82 I lift my eyes to the mountains;
    where is my help to come from?
  Help comes to me from Yahweh God,
    who made heaven and earth.

  No letting our footsteps slip!
    This guard of yours does not doze!
  The guardian of Israel
    does not doze or sleep.

  Yahweh God guards you, shades you.
    With Yahweh at your right hand
  sun cannot strike you down by day,
    nor moon at night.

  Yahweh God guards you from harm,
    God guards your lives,
  Yahweh guards your leaving, coming back,
    now and for always.

  The Holy Bible, Psalm 121 (Jerusalem Bible, adapted)

83 Lord our God and God of our forebears, help us live according to your teaching and to hold fast to your commands. Let
   us not come into the power of sin or wrong-doing, temptation or disgrace. Let no evil within us control us, and keep us
   far from bad people and bad company. Help us hold fast to
   the good within us and to good deeds, and bend our will
   and our desires to serve you. Give us today, and every day,
   grace, kindness and mercy in your sight and in the sight of
   all who regard us, and grant us your love and kindness.
   Blessed are you Lord, who grant love and kindness to your
   people Israel.   11

   from the Daily Morning Service (Reform Synagogues of GB)

84 I have no other helper than you,
no other father,
no other redeemer,
no other support.
I pray to you.
Only you can help me.
My present misery
is too great.
Despair grips me,
and I am at my wits' end.
I am sunk in the depths,
and I cannot pull myself up
or out.
If it is your will,
help me out of this misery.
Let me know
that you are stronger
than all misery and all enemies.
O Lord, if I come through this,
please let the experience
contribute to my and my brothers' blessing.
You will not forsake me;
this I know.   25
Amen.

Ghana

85 Good God of this earth, my Lord,
you are above me, I am below.
When misfortunes comes to me,
just as the trees keep off the sun from me
so may you take away misfortune.
My Lord, be my shadow.

Calling on you, I pass the day;
calling on you, I pass the night.
When the moon rises, do not forget me;
when I rise, I do not forget you.
Let the danger pass me by:
God, my Lord, you sun with thirty rays.

God, you hold the bad and the good in your hand;
my Lord, do not allow us to be killed,
we, your little ones, are praying to you.

A person who doesn't know the difference between good
   and bad cannot make you angry;
once he does know and is unwilling to behave
   accordingly,
this is wicked – treat him as you think fit.

God, you made all the animals and people
that live upon the earth;
also, the corn on the earth where we live –
you made that too; we have not made it.
You have given us strength.
You have given us cattle and corn.

We worked the land and the seed grew up for us.
People were satisfied
with the corn which you allowed to grow for us.
The corn in the house has been burnt up;
who has burnt the corn in the house?
You know who it was.

You have allowed all this to be done;
why have you done this?
You know.
You show before our eyes
the corn which you allowed to grow.
The hungry look at it and are comforted.

When the corn blooms you send butterflies
and locusts into it – locusts and doves.
All this comes from your hand.
Have you caused this to happen?
Why have you done this?
You know why.

If you love me
set me free, I beg you from my heart;
if I do not pray to you from my heart
you do not hear me.
If I pray to you with my heart,
you know it and you are kind to me.   36, 31

Boran, Kenya

86 Happy is the person
who never takes the advice of wicked people,
or spends time in the places that sinners frequent
or sits around with people
who mock and ridicule others.
Happy is the person
who is content with doing what Yahweh God wants.
Happy is the person
who reflects on the law of Yahweh God at prayer,
day and night.

Yahweh God will protect that person.
But God help the wicked!

The Holy Bible: Psalm 1

87 Controller of existence, and Lord of lords, we do not rely on
our own good deeds but on your great mercy as we lay our
needs before you. Lord, hear! Lord, pardon! Lord, listen and
act! What are we? What is our life? What is our love? What is
our justice? What is our success? What is our endurance?
What is our power? Lord our God, and God of our forebears,
what can we say before you, for in your presence are not the
powerful as nothing, the famous as if they had never existed, the learned as if without knowledge, and the intelli-
gent as if without insight. To you most of our actions are
pointless and our daily life is shallow. Even the superiority
of humans over the beasts is nothing. For everything is
trivial except the pure soul which must one day give its
account and reckoning before the judgment seat of your
glory.   11

from the Daily Morning Service (Reform Synagogues of GB)

88 For you shall go out with joy
and be led forth with peace.
The mountains and the hills
shall break forth into singing.
Therefore with joy shall you draw water
from the wells of salvation.
Cry aloud and shout, O inhabitant of Zion.
Hallelujah!   11

from The Holy Book, Isaiah 55: 12; 12: 3, 6

89 Buyers and sellers,
  God, you know, in our country these people are quite
    special,
  but nobody can fool you, neither the buyer nor those
    who sell.
  It is not just a trifle over which we can make merry.
  There can be fraud whilst people are hungry.
  Others pile up their riches.
  God, whether we buy or sell, let us stick to this.
  We are quite willing to pay the value of the goods,
  but others should not overcharge.
  God, make peace here as well.
  Amen   26

  Ghana

90 Creator, where shall I find you?
  High and hidden is your place.
  And where shall I not find you?
  The world is full of your glory.

  I have sought your nearness,
  with all my heart I called you
  and going out to meet you
  I found you coming to meet me.   11

  Judah Halevi

91 The Lord's my shepherd, I'll not want,
  he makes me down to lie, in pastures green;
  he leadeth me the quiet waters by.
  My soul he doth restore again;
  and me to walk doth make within the paths of
    righteousness,
  ev'n for his own name's sake.

  Yea, though I walk in death's dark vale, yet
  will I fear none ill: for thou art with me
  and thy rod and staff me comfort still.
  My table thou hast furnished
  in presence of my foes; my head thou dost with oil
    anoint,
  and my cup overflows.

Goodness and mercy all my life
shall surely follow me;
and in God's house for evermore
my dwelling place shall be.

The Holy Bible: Psalm 23

92 In the days to come, the mountain of the Temple of Yahweh
God shall tower above the other mountains and be lifted
higher than the hills. All the nations will come to it; people
without number will come to it, and they will say:

'Come, let us go up to the mountain of Yahweh,
to the Temple of the God of Jacob,
so that God may teach us new ways
and we may walk in new paths.

God will rule over all the peoples
and judge between them;
they will take their weapons of death
and make them into farming tools.

People will no longer fight with each other,
and no one will begin training for war.
O my people, come,
let us walk in the light of Yahweh, the Lord.'

The Holy Bible: Isaiah 2 (Jerusalem Bible, adapted)

93 O God, you have let me pass the night in peace,
let me pass the day in peace.
Wherever I may go upon my way
which you made peaceable for me,
O God, lead my steps.
When I have spoken, keep lies away from me.
When I am hungry, keep me from murmuring.
When I am satisfied, keep me from pride.
Calling upon you, I pass the day,
O Lord, who has no Lord.   32

Boran, Kenya

94 God has turned his back on us;
   the words of men have made him angry.
   And yet he will turn round again.
   God has turned his back on us.
   We are the children of our Maker
   and are not afraid that he will kill us.   23

   Dinka, Sudan

95 We have a strong city; to guard us God has surrounded us
   with walls and earthworks. Open the gates! Let the honest
   peoples come in. Welcome the faithful nation who looks for
   peace and who trusts in you, O God. Trust in Yahweh
   forever, for God is the everlasting rock.

   Yahweh God has brought low those who lived high up in
   the defended town. God brings it crashing down to the
   ground, and flings it down in the dust. And now the feet of
   the poor and those who have nothing will trample on it.
   Yahweh God alone is our everlasting rock.

   The path of the honest person is straight; you, Lord, make
   the path smooth. We followed in your paths, Lord, and we
   put all our hope in you, Yahweh. At night my soul is waiting
   for you and my spirit is looking for you. When you come to
   judge the earth, people will understand the meaning of
   honesty.

   If good things happen for the wicked, they do not learn
   the importance of honesty. They continue to do wicked
   things, and forget about the goodness of God. O God, your
   hand is raised in judgment, but the wicked do not see it. Let
   them see your love, and be ashamed of their wickedness.

   Yahweh God, you are giving us peace, because you treat
   us as our deeds deserve. Yahweh our God, other rulers than
   you have ruled over us. But we do not recognise any other
   ruler except you. We do not acknowledge any other name
   than yours.

   from The Holy Bible: Isaiah 26

96. Our Father, it is your universe,
it is your will, let us be at peace;
let the souls of your people be cool;
you are our Father,
remove all evil from our path.   8

Nuer, Sudan

97 Therefore, Lord our God, we put our hope in you. Soon let
us witness the glory of your power; when the worship of
material things shall pass away from the earth, and prejudice and superstition shall at last be cut off; when the
world will be set right by the rule of God, and all humankind
shall speak out in your name, and all the wicked of the earth
shall turn to you. Then all who inhabit this world shall meet
in understanding, and shall know that to you alone every
one shall submit, and pledge themselves in every tongue. In
your presence, Lord our God, they shall bow down and be
humble, honouring the glory of your being. All shall accept
the duty of building your kingdom, so that your reign of
goodness shall come soon and last forever. For yours alone is
the true kingdom, and only the glory of your rule endures
forever. So it is written in your Torah:
    'The Lord shall rule forever and ever.'
So it is prophesied:
    'The Lord shall be as a king over all the earth.
    On that day the Lord shall be One, and known as One.'
                                                 11

from the Sabbath Evening Service (Reform Synagogues of GB)

Trials and disasters Famine and drought

98 God of our ancestors,
I lie down without food,
I lie down hungry,
although others have eaten and lie down full.
Even if it be but a polecat or a little rock-rabbit,
give me and I shall be grateful.
I cry to God, Ancestor of my ancestors.   33

Barolong, South Africa

99 My God, have mercy on our children
who were late in getting up.
My God, do not lead our children to ruin.
My God, our life is in our children.
My God, give us children, both small and big.
My God, be the guardian of our children
that are away in order to feed our cattle
in any grassland.
My God, I am old and near death
and my house needs help.
You be the guardian of all creatures.
Let it be so, my God.
Answer kindly to the words that we,
a group of elders, have said to you.
And God answered affirmatively.   29

Samburu, Kenya

100 Heart return to the place. The seeker of the thing has found
it. Drawer, bring the little bud of the water of the rain. God
send us a great spreading rain, that the little boys may eat for
themselves the herbs and salad plants of the deserted
homesteads.   3

South Africa?

101 O Chief who have left me in this world at your death,
I come to offer the sacrifices.
Rain has ceased to fall in our country long ago.
Give us rain! Here is your water!
Give us rain! Let it rain!
Why do you leave me in trouble, you my Lord?
I have inherited your power. I did not usurp it.
You have left me in trouble.
If you continue and it does not rain in the land,
the inhabitants will go away.
Look, here is the goat, and here is your sheep!   32

Nyamwezi, Tanzania

102 In you, God, I take shelter,
let me never be disgraced.
In your justice deliver me,
hear me and speedily rescue me.

Be a sheltering rock for me,
a mighty stronghold to save me.
For you are my rock, my stronghold,
for your name's sake, guide me, lead me!

Release me from the net they have spread out for me,
because you are my safety.
Into your hands I entrust my spirit,
you will save me, Yahweh God.

O God of truth, you hate those
who worship false and empty idols;
But I put my trust in you Yahweh.
I will be glad and rejoice in your love.

You who have seen my wretchedness
and know the miseries of my soul.
You have not handed me over to the enemy
but you have given my feet space to roam.

73

Take pity on me, God,
I am in trouble now.
Grief wastes away my eyes,
my throat and my inner parts.

My life is worn out with sorrow,
my years with sighs;
my strength yields under misery,
my bones are wasting away.

But I put my trust in you, Yahweh,
I say: 'You are my God'.
My days are in your hand, rescue me
From the hands of my enemies and persecutors.
Let your face smile on your servant,
save me in your love.

from The Holy Bible: Psalm 31 (Jerusalem Bible, adapted)

103 Here is your cow, your food.
We pray to [Kyala]. May theft go away.
Give us food and beans and millet,
may we eat and be satisfied . . .
It is said that the sweet potatoes are scarce now, help us.
You [Mwakabule, Mwakomo] . . . This is your cow,
    [Mwaijonga].
This is your meat.
I shall seek another also which we shall give you like
    this.
May the locusts go away.
It is you who have caused theft because there is hunger.
At night, since we eat scraps of food our bellies are
    disquieted . . .
May we be satisfied.
People are eating millet porridge;
when food is plentiful they say it's horrible.
When someone eats millet porridge he dies, it kills a
    man.
We pray to him, this Kyala, because we do not know
    him,
so we say: 'You [Mwaijonga] drive away the hunger.
Give all of us, [Mwaipopo's] people, food
and hear us all.'   39

Nyakyusa, Tanzania

04 Save me, O God, for the water is already up to my neck. I
have sunk into the deepest swamp, and there is no foothold.
I have fallen into deep water, and the waves are breaking
over me. I am tired out with shouting; my throat is hoarse;
my eyes are strained.

There are more people that hate me for no reason, than I
have hairs on my head. God, you know how foolish I have
been; my offences are not hidden from you. But let those
who put their trust in you not blush to see me, Lord; let them
not be ashamed of me.

Pull me out of this swamp; let me sink no further. Let me
escape those who hate me. Do not let the deep water
swallow me, or the pit close its mouth on me. In your loving
kindness, answer me, Yahweh; turn to me in your great
tenderness.

My shame and disgrace are past curing. I had hoped for
sympathy, but in vain, I found no one of any comfort to me.
They gave me poison to eat, and when I was thirsty they
gave me vinegar to drink. God, let your anger overtake
them, for adding to my wounds.

For myself, wounded wretch that I am, by your saving
power, God, lift me up! I will praise your name with a song,
then when they see this the humble can rejoice. Long life to
all those who seek God. God will always hear those who are
in need.

from The Holy Bible: Psalm 69

05 You who give sustenance to your creatures, O God,
Put water for us in the nipples of rain!

You who poured water into oceans, O God,
Make this land of ours fertile again!

Accepter of penance, who are wealthy, O God,
Gather water in rivers whose beds have run dry!

You who are steadfast and act justly, O God,
Provide us with what we want you to grant!

You who are glorious, truly bounteous, O God,
Our cries have undone us, grant a shower of rain!

You who are clement, truly worshipped, O God,
Milk water for beasts which are stricken with thirst!

Creator of nature who made all things, O God,
Transmute our ruin to blessing and good!

Eternal rewarder of merits, O God,
Let that rain come which people used to drink!

We have done much Remembrance, O God who
   remember,
Loosen upon us rain from the clouds!

You who are merciful and compassionate, O God,
Milk rain from the sky for those in need!

Giver of victuals at all times, O God,
Who can do what you want, bestow on us rain!

You who are peace and a curtain, O God,
Provide us with what we want you to grant!

Recorder of merit, who requite us, O God,
Into scorched empty ponds pour us water of rain!

You who are truthful, creator, O God,
We accept in submission whatever you say!

You who mete out good and evil, O God,
In this land we are broken, milk the clouds from above!

The earth and the sky you constructed, O God,
We cannot get water, bring forth drops of rain!

The darkness of night you transfigure, O God,
And make daylight follow; milk the sky lavishly!

You who gave brightness to sunshine, O God,
And know its principles, give us brown water from rain!

You who are rich and ward off cares, O God,
Milk temperate rain! help us with rain everywhere!

You who open all and give sustenance, O God,
People have scattered; send forth healthy rain!

Almighty, perfector of counsels, O God,
Pour for us rain which would make the land wet!

You who are bounteous, the protector, O God,
We cannot survive drought, send us rain from your
   store!

You who drive the air which sways the trees, O God,
It is you whom we praised, grant us the goodness of
   rain!

You who are worshipped and answer prayers, O God,
Make the rain spread over the whole of the land!

Bestower of victories, benefactor, O God,
Bring us faultless rain which makes us dwell where it
   falls!

You who are one and are trusted, O God,
Provider of all, give water to your people!

You who spark off lightning from clouds you have
   loaded, O God,
It is you who have power over rain which satisfies
   abundantly!

You who fill water-holes dug in wadis, O God,
Milk rain on this land, cream-giving rain!

Who used to relieve the strangest plights, O God,
It is to you that I have turned for help!   10

Somali, Somalia

06 The source of being is above,
   which gives life to all people;
   For people are satisfied, and do not die of famine,
   For the Lord gives them life,
   that they may live prosperously
   on the earth and not die of famine.   21

   Zulu, South Africa

07 All our forebears, come and eat kola.
   All those who gave us birth, come and hear.
   Quell the quarrel,
   quell the hot exchange of words.
   We are not the first to err, neither the last.
   This is your white hen and these are the yams.
   The mistake has been made;
   it will not happen again.
   Avert this evil. Avert this evil. Avert this evil.
   The invisible spirits that molest us,
   eat this and be appeased.   1

   Ibo, Nigeria

108 Alleluia!
Let my whole being give praise to the Lord.
I intend to give him praise all my life.
I promise to sing his praises as long as I live.

Do not put your trust in people, in power,
or in any other person – they cannot save you;
everyone will die sooner or later, and return to dust.
So, when people die, that will be the end of all their
    plans.

If you put your trust in God, then you will be happy,
and if your hope is in the Lord, you will be all right.
God made the earth and the whole world,
and the seas and everything there is.

Yahweh God is always worthy of trust,
God will always support those who are oppressed.
God will provide food for the hungry
and set free those unjustly imprisoned.

Yahweh God will cure the blind,
God will heal the crippled.
Our God is the protector of strangers,
and God will support the orphan and the widowed.

Yahweh God loves those who try to be good,
and sooner or later God will punish the wicked.
Our God rules forever and ever,
God will never end; Yahweh will support us.

The Holy Bible: Psalm 146

Blessings

9 Blessed be he, who gives rest to his people Israel on the holy Sabbath day.

Blessed be he, and blessed be his name.

Blessed be the knowledge of him for all eternity.

Blessed are you, Lord our God, king of the universe, the king, great and holy; merciful father, praised by his people; worshipped and glorified by the tongue of all who love and serve him. Therefore we praise you, Lord our God, with the psalms of your servant David; with prayers and songs we declare your glory, your greatness, your splendour, and your majesty. We proclaim your name, our king, our God, who alone is the life of all existence, and whose name is worshipped and glorified forever and ever. Blessed are you Lord, the king praised in all worship.   11

from Sabbath Morning Service (Reform Synagogues of GB)

10 BLESSINGS CONCERNING EVENTS

On hearing bad news
Blessed are you, Lord our God, creator of the universe, the true judge.

On hearing news which is good for you and for others
Blessed are you, Lord our God, creator of the universe, who is good and does good.

On seeing one who has recovered from serious illness
Blessed is the all-merciful, creator of the universe, who has restored you to us and not to the dust.

On seeing a place where a wondeful thing happened to you
Blessed are you, Lord our God, creator of the universe, who performed a wonderful thing for me at this place.   11

Jewish prayers

111 BLESSINGS CONCERNING PEOPLE

On seeing people of unusual appearance
Blessed are you, Lord our God, king of the universe, who varies the forms of creation.

On seeing kings and rulers
Blessed are you, Lord our God, king of the universe, who has given of his glory to flesh and blood.

On seeing people with religious knowledge and wisdom
Blessed are you, Lord our God, king of the universe, who has given a share of his wisdom to those in awe of him.   11

Jewish Prayers

112 *When people are handed the fire at the end of the ceremony they are blessed with these words.*

Receive this holy fire.
Make your lives like this fire.
A holy life that is seen.
A life of God that is seen.
A life that has no end.
A life that darkness does not overcome.
May this light of God in you grow.
Light a fire that is worthy of your heads.
Light a fire that is worthy of your children.
Light a fire that is worthy of your fathers.
Light a fire that is worthy of your mothers.
Light a fire that is worthy of God.
Now go in peace.
**May the Almighty protect you
today and all days.**   27

Masai, Tanzania

13 Wherever you go, I will go;
wherever you live I will live.
Your people shall be my people,
and your God, my God.
Wherever you die I will die
and there I will be buried.
May Yahweh God do this thing to me
and more also
if even death should come between us.

The Holy Bible: Ruth 1:16-17 (Jerusalem Bible)

14 May God raise you up
above everything.
Spread out like water of a lake.
Be abundance that never ends,
that never changes.
Be like a mountain.
Be like a camel.
Be like a cloud –
a cloud that brings rain always.
And God promised that it would be so.   29

Samburu, Kenya

15 BLESSINGS CONCERNING NATURE

On seeing the wonders of nature
Blessed are you, Lord our God, creator of the universe, who
performs the work of creation.

For thunder
Blessed are you, Lord our God, creator of the universe,
whose strength and power fill the world.

On seeing a rainbow
Blessed are you, Lord our God, creator of the universe, who
remembers his covenant and is faithful to it, and keeps his
promise.

On seeing the sea
Blessed are you, Lord our God, creator of the universe, who
made the great sea.

On seeing the beauties of nature
Blessed are you, Lord our God, creator of the universe, who
has such as these in your world.   11

Jewish prayers

116 GOD'S ELECTION AND HIS FAVOUR

'If Yahweh set his heart on you and chose you, it was not
because you outnumbered other peoples: you were the least
of all peoples. It was for love of you and to keep the oath he
swore to your fathers that Yahweh brought you out with his
mighty hand and redeemed you from the house of slavery,
from the power of Pharaoh king of Egypt. Know then that
Yahweh your God is God indeed, the faithful God who is
true to his covenant and his graciousness for a thousand
generations towards those who love him and keep his
commandments, but who punishes in their own persons
those that hate him. He is not slow to destroy the man who
hates him; he makes him work out his punishment in
person. You are therefore to keep and observe the commandments and statutes and ordinances that I lay down for
you today.
    'Listen to these ordinances, be true to them and observe
them, and in return Yahweh your God will be true to the
covenant and the kindness he promised your father solemn-
ly. He will love you and bless you and increase your numbers; he will bless the fruit of your body and the produce of
your soil, your corn, your wine, your oil, the issue of your
cattle, the young of your flock, in the land he swore to your
fathers he would give you. You will be more blessed than all
peoples. No man or woman among you shall be barren, no
male or female of your beasts infertile. Yahweh will keep all
sickness far from you; he will not afflict you with those evil
plagues of Egypt which you have known, but will save them
for all those who hate you.'

The Holy Bible: Deuteronomy 7:7-15 (Jerusalem Bible)

117 The Lord does rule, the Lord has ruled, the Lord shall rule
forever and ever.
    The Lord shall be as a king over the whole earth. On that
day the Lord shall be One, and known as One.

Save us, Lord our God, to proclaim your holy name and be honoured in praising you.

Blessed is the Lord God of Israel from everlasting to everlasting. Let all the people say: Amen! Praise the Lord!

May all who live praise the Lord. Hallelujah!　　　　11

from Sabbath Morning Service (Reform Synagogues of GB)

8 Blessed be the Lord forever. Amen and amen.

Blessed be the Lord God, the God of Israel, who alone works wonders.

Blessed be the Lord's glorious name forever. All the earth is full of God's glory. Amen and amen.　　　　11

from Sabbath Morning Service (Reform Synagogues of GB)

19 May the people bless your glorious name, though it is beyond all blessing and praise. You are the Lord alone; you made the sky, the reaches of space and its countless lights, the earth and everything on it, the seas and everything in them; you give life to them all, and the universe worships you.

The Holy Bible: Nehemiah 9:5-6

20 KING DAVID'S BLESSING

'Blessed are you Lord, the God of our father Israel from everlasting to everlasting. Yours is the greatness, the power, the splendour, the glory and the majesty, for everything in heaven and earth is yours. Yours is the kingdom and you are exalted supreme over all. Wealth and honour come from you, for you rule over all. In your hand are strength and might. It is in your power to give greatness and strength to all. And now, our God, we give you thanks and praise your glorious name.'

The Holy Bible: 1 Chronicles 29:11-13

21 May God go with you!

Go nicely: may your path be swept [of danger].
God go with you, and may you be left [escape from] the mishaps ahead!

May you go with God!

Let God bear you in peace like a young shoot!

May you meet with the Kindly-disposed One!

May God take care of you!

May God walk you well!

May you pass the night with God!

May you remain with God!

May God be with you who remain behind!

May you stay with God!   21

Various African blessings

122 May the rising sun expose all wicked people.
     . . . East, I invoke your presence;
     West, I call upon you too.
     O Heaven, your attention please.
     I also invoke the presence of your beloved (spouse)
        Earth.
     [Mawu,] God, the Almighty, The Great Creator,
     who makes the hands and the feet,
     I fervently invoke your presence.
     . . . Grandmother, I invoke your presence . . .
     Attention please . . .
     I am only an ignorant child before you.
     All Chiefs and Elders, peace be with you,
     grant that all misfortunes return whither they rightly
        belong.
     May our world know only peace.
     Grant good health to all your male servants.
     Grant good health to all your female servants too.
     Grant that our ears hear only the message of life,
     and our eyes see only that which is life-giving.
     Give us good health.
     Do not allow us to be confined to the heat of the sick
        bed,
     but grant that we bask forever outside in the rays
     of the life-giving sun.
     Whenever both your male and female servants engage in
        any venture

                              84

please remove all difficulty from their way,
that they succeed abundantly . . .
Bless those who have no children, with plenty of
    children,
and grant an increase to those who already have
    children.
Grant good health to the farmer,
that his hoe may find enough work to do
and the harvest far outweigh his labour.
When the fisherman goes out in his canoe
grant that he direct his canoe to where the fish are,
that his net may have a good catch.
Grant that the catch may safely reach home.
Please drive away all kinds of inedible fish
and allow us to catch only the edible, and very
    plentifully.
Help our traders too, that they may succeed in all that
    they do.
Indeed, whatever your male and female servants do,
let your presence be with them always.
Let no one die prematurely.
It is for good health that we pray.
Grant that all manner of misfortunes may be far from us.
From his sons and daughters the buffalo drives away all
    poverty as year succeeds year.
Worship should never (consist of) events to be counted.
Grant a constant good health to all . . .
To the masons and the carpenters grant increased skill in
    their work.
To the traders grant success when they set out with their
    wares.
Good health to all.
Long life and prosperity to all.   12

Anlo Ewe, Ghana

23 Thank you Father for your free gift of fire.
    Because it is through fire that you draw near to us every
        day.
    It is with fire that you constantly bless us.
    Our Father, bless this fire today.
    With your power enter into it.
    Make this fire a worthy thing.

A thing that carries your blessing.
Let it become a reminder of your love.
A reminder of life without end.
Make the life of these people to be baptised like this fire.
A thing that shines for the sake of people.
A thing that shines for your sake.
Father, heed this sweet smelling smoke.
Make their life also sweet smelling.
A thing sweet smelling that rises to God.
A holy thing.
A thing fitting for you.   27

Masai, Tanzania

124 May Yahweh God bless you and keep you.
     May Yahweh God let his face shine on you and be
        gracious to you.
     May Yahweh God uncover his face to you and bring you
        peace.
     The Holy Bible: Numbers 6:24-26 (Jerusalem Bible)

125 BLESSINGS CONCERNING FOOD

     For fruits which grow on trees
     Blessed are you, God, ruler of the universe, who creates the
     fruit of the tree.

     For vegetables
     Blessed are you, God, ruler of the universe, who creates the
     fruit of the earth.

     For all other food
     Blessed are you, God, ruler of the universe, by whose word
     all things exist.

     After eating any food except bread
     Blessed are you, God, ruler of the universe, who creates
     many living things and their needs, with all that you created
     to keep each one of them alive. Blessed are you, the life of all
     existence.   11

     Jewish prayers

6 BLESSINGS AT MEALS

Ladies and gentlemen, let us say grace.
All reply
Blessed be the name of the Lord from now and forever.

With your permission, let us bless our God whose food
we have eaten.
All reply
Blessed be the Lord our God whose food we have eaten, and
through whose goodness we live.
Blessed be God, and blessed be God's name.
Blessed are you, Lord our God, ruler of the universe, who
feeds the whole world through your goodness, with grace,
kindness and mercy. You give food to all flesh, for your love
is forever. Through your great goodness food has never
failed us, and may it never fail us because of your greatness;
for you feed and provide for all and do good to all, and
prepare food for all your creatures that you have created.
Blessed are you Yahweh God who give food to all.

Our God, our father, be our shepherd and feed us, provide
for us, sustain us and support us, and relieve us speedily
from all our troubles. Let us never be in need of the charity of
our fellowmen and women nor their loans, but dependent
on your hand alone which is full, open, holy and ample, so
shall we never lose our self-respect nor be put to shame.

Blessed are you, Lord our God, king of the universe; the God
who is our father, our king, our source of power, our creator,
our redeemer, our maker, our Holy One, the Holy One of
Jacob; our shepherd, the shepherd of Israel, the good king
who does good to all. Every day he has done good, does
good and will do good for us. Generously he has provided
for us, he does provide for us and always will provide for us
grace, kindness, mercy and relief, deliverance and prosperity, blessing and salvation, consolation, provision and support, mercy, life, peace and all good. Let us never be in want
of any goodness. [11]

Jewish prayers

127 BLESSING AFTER A MEAL

The All-merciful, may he rule over us forever and ever.

The All-merciful, may he be blessed in heaven and on earth.

The All-merciful, may he be praised through all generations, glorified among us for eternity, and honoured among us forever.

The All-merciful, may he give us an honourable livelihood.

The All-merciful, may he break off the yoke from our neck, and lead us with uprightness to our land.

The All-merciful, may he send a plentiful blessing on this house, and on this table at which we have eaten.   11

Jewish Prayer

128 May we stay well in this country; we did not know that we would arrive here. May we stay with peace and dream honey [i.e. may we have pleasant dreams]; the God of old, the Sun, when it rises in the East, may it bring us honey, and when it goes to set in the West may it take the badness with it.   21

Nyole (Abaluyia), Kenya

129 If you live according to my laws, if you keep my commandments and put them into practice, I will give you the rain you need at the right time; the earth shall give its produce and the trees of the countryside their fruits; you shall thresh until vintage time and gather grapes until sowing time. You shall eat your fill of bread and live secure in your land.

I will give peace to the land, and you shall sleep with none to frighten you. I will rid the land of beasts of prey. The sword shall not pass through your land.

I will turn towards you, I will make you be fruitful and multiply, and I will uphold my Covenant with you.

You shall eat your fill of last year's harvest, and still throw out the old to make room for the new.

I will set up my dwelling among you, and I will not cast you off. I will live in your midst; I will be your God and you shall be my people. It is I, Yahweh your God, who have brought you out of the land of Egypt so that you should be

their servants no longer. I have broken the yoke that bound
you and have made you walk with head held high.

The Holy Bible: Leviticus 26:3-13 (Jerusalem Bible)

130 Bless this tree; make it grow; let it be entirely a blessing
without any evil. Remove all evil; let it not come but let only
the good come. Give your blessing that we may increase in
all things and grow in plenty and be free from disease. Let
blessings abound. 21

Banyoro, Uganda

131 Spread out . . . all your days.
May your children and cattle be plentiful
like down of lichens clinging to citron trees on the
  mountains.
Be fragrant like a fragrant resin.
May God grant you to last a long time . . .
May you have a fragrance of sweet life always, without
  end. 29

Samburu, Kenya

132 Blessed be God, at whose word the world existed.
Blessed be God, whose word is deed.
Blessed be God, whose command stands firm.
Blessed be God, who makes creation.
Blessed be God, who has mercy on the earth.
Blessed be God, who has mercy on all creatures.
Blessed be God, who gives a good reward to those in
  awe of him.
Blessed be God, who takes away darkness and brings on
  light.
Blessed be God, who lives forever and exists for eternity.
Blessed be God, who has no fault and no forgetfulness,
  who shows no favour and takes no bribe. Righteous is
  God in every way and loving in every deed.
Blessed be God, who redeems and rescues. 11

from Sabbath Morning Service (Reform Synagogues of GB)

133 **My God, the soul you have given me is pure**, for you created it, **you formed it and you made it live within me.** You watch over it within me, but one day you will take it from me to everlasting life. My God and God of my ancestors, as long as the soul is within me, I will declare that you are the master of all deeds, the ruler of all creatures and the Lord of every soul. Blessed are you God, who brings the dead into everlasting life.

Blessed are you, Lord our God, creator of the universe, who frees those who are bound.

Blessed are you, Lord our God, creator of the universe, who lifts up those bent low.

Blessed are you, Lord our God, creator of the universe, who provides for my every need.

Blessed are you, Lord our God, creator of the universe, who **strengthens our steps.**

Blessed are you, Lord our God, creator of the universe, who crowns Israel with glory.

Blessed are you, Lord our God, creator of the universe, who gives strength to the weary.

Blessed are you, Lord our God, creator of the universe, who takes away sleep from my eyes and slumber from my eyelids. 11

from Daily Morning Service (Reform Synagogues of GB)

134 May the God bless you and keep you.
May the face of the God enlighten you and be gracious to you.
May the God turn towards you and give you peace. 11

from Sabbath Evening Service (Reform Synagogues of GB)

135 BLESSING A NEW HOUSE

May those who are going to live in this house have many children; may they be honest to the people and good to the poor; may they not suffer from disease or any other kind of trouble; may they be safe all these years. 21

Nyole (Abaluyia), Kenya

5 Naked I came from my mother's womb,
naked I shall return.
Yahweh gave; Yahweh has taken back;
blessed be the name of Yahweh.

The Holy Bible: Job 1:21 (Jerusalem Bible)

7 May God grant you a tranquil night.
May God support you during the day.
May God grant you shadow in the evening
and in the morning,
all your days.   29

Samburu, Kenya

38 PROCREATION BLESSINGS

You want fruit: may God give you fruit!

May God give you many children!   21

39 My God, grant me a life that never ceases.
My God, may I always spread out.
My God, destroy hatreds that hate me.
My God, may I proceed with a life that endures
through generations, both living and not living.
Grant me, then, God, to always rise
higher and higher.
And God said: 'All right'.   29

Samburu, Kenya

40 The Lord does rule, the Lord has ruled, the Lord shall rule
forever and ever.
   The Lord shall be as a king over the whole earth. On that
day the Lord shall be One, and known as One.
   Save us, Lord our God, to proclaim your holy name and be
honoured in praising you.
   Blessed is the Lord God of Israel from everlasting to
everlasting. Let all the people say: Amen! praise the Lord!
   May all who live praise the Lord. Hallelujah!   11

from Sabbath Morning Service (Reform Synagogues of GB)

141 Peace and welcome to you, servants of the Lord, messengers
of the Most High, of the King above the kings of kings, the
Holy One, blessed be he.

Enter in peace, you servants of peace, messengers of the
Most High, of the King above the kings of kings, the Holy
One, blessed be he.

Bless me with peace, you servants of peace, messengers of
the Most High, of the King above the kings of kings, the
Holy One, blessed be he.

Go forth in peace, you servants of peace, messengers of
the Most High, of the King above the kings of kings, the
Holy One, blessed be he.   11

from Sabbath Eve Home Service (Reform Synagogues of GB)

9

Women Mothers and children

Leader Thou, [Jouk,] God, who art our Father and hast
created all of us,
thou knowest that this women is ours,
and we wish her to bear children –

All Grant children to her!

Leader Should we die tomorrow, no children of ours
will remain –

All Grant children to her!

Leader If she bears a son,
his name will be the name of his grandfather.
If she bears a daughter,
her name will be the name of her grandmother.

All Grant children to her!

Leader Would it be displeasing to thee if many children
surrounded us?
Spirit of the father,
spirit of the grandfather,
you who dwell now in the skies,
are you displeased that we ask for children?

All Grant children to her!

Leader Should we die without them, who will guard
the family?
Your name and ours shall be forgotten upon the
earth.

All   **Grant us this night good dreams,**
          that we will die leaving many children behind
          us.   23

    Giur, Sudan

143 O Mother, we beseech thee to deliver us;
     look after us,
     look after our children.   16

    Yoruba, Nigeria

144 O [Imana,] God of Urundi,
     if only you would help me!
     O Imana of pity,
     God of my father's house,
     if only you would help me!
     O Imana of the country of the Hutu and Tutsi,
     if only you would help me just this once!
     O God, if only you would give me
     a homestead and children!
     I prostrate myself before you,
     God of Urundi.
     I cry to you: give me offspring,
     give me as you give to others!
     Imana, what shall I do, where shall I go?
     I am in distress,
     where is there room for me?
     O merciful, O Imana of mercy,
     help this once.   13, 31

    Hutu and Tutsi, Burundi

145 O God, thou art great,
     thou art the One who created me,
     I have no other.
     God, thou art in the heavens,
     thou art the only one:
     now my child is sick,
     and thou wilt grant my desire.   21

    Anuak, Sudan

46 God agrees: let us pray to God.
When I pray for this woman, God, agree with us.
God, do not be annoyed.
God, let her not die, this woman;
do not take her away from her children.
God, grant her to guide them.
God, agree to this.
God, grant that she may still remain
together with her children:
do not take her away from all of us, this mother.
God, who give us rain, do not take this mother from us.
Give us back her spirit: give it back to us,
for us and for her children, and for her mother,
and for this group of elders, so many of them,
and for all who intercede for this woman.
God, agree with us.   29

Samburu, Kenya

47 You, ancestors causing this difficult birth,
support our sister during her labour.
We bring you this chicken and this flour.
We beg you! Our lips are dry like dead leaves.
Help us, so that she may safely deliver her child.
The proverb says: where there are men there are axes,
wherever there are men they split and multiply.
Those who are born and those who remain after us
will remain to pay you honour.
But if you act like this, will there be anyone left
to pay you honour?
Help us now, so that she delivers a healthy baby,
in such a way that her womb may be refreshed.
Accept this chicken and this flour.
And you, God on high, we beg you: have pity on us.
See how our lips are dried up in our mouths.
We are begging you, Lord, help us,
so that your man-child may be saved,
and so that our hearts may rest easy.
Have pity on this little child, and on every little child
that is giving increase to the world.
What good will be served if this present situation
results in death?
We are begging you, Ancestors, and Lord God.   6

Tutshiokwé, Congo

148 THE MOTHER'S PRAYER

Father of all mankind, and source of all life, through your great love I enter your house to thank you and to bless your name. You have given me the joy of creation, which supported me in my weakness, and comforted me in my anxiety. Your mercy has restored me. I thank you for my life and for the life of my child, for you renew the wonder of creation.

For an adopted child
Father of all mankind, and source of all life, through your great love I enter your house to thank you and to bless your name. I give you thanks for you have found me worthy. I turn to you in awe because you have put your trust in me. I bless you for the love which binds me to my child; and for the wonder of creation which you have renewed within my heart.

For a boy
As he grows in body and in mind, may the law of truth be found on his lips and the love of justice in his heart. May he be a blessing to those around him and bring honour to Israel in the sight of all mankind.

Lord, be with me and my husband; may our love for our child draw us even more closely together in helpfulness and in trust.

Teach us to carry on through our child the heritage of Israel, so that its tradition of wisdom and holiness may never cease.

Now in love we comfort him; may he comfort us in future years. Amen.

For a girl
As she grows in body and in mind, may the law of truth be found on her lips and the love of justice in her heart. May she be a blessing to those around her and bring honour to Israel in the sight of all mankind.

Lord, be with me and my husband; may our love for our child draw us even more closely together in helpfulness and in trust.

Teach us to carry on through our child the heritage of Israel, so that its tradition of wisdom and holiness may never cease.

Now in love we comfort her; may she comfort us in future
years. Amen.   11

Thanksgiving Service for Parents (Reform Synagogues of GB)

9 God, Supreme Being, Lord,
may I and my children become extremely strong
like the ant and the blacksmith's hammer, like the iron
    in the forge.
May the jealous man not stretch out his hand against us.
May the witch die by that death which he deals out to
    others.
You, water which gives salt to the earth,
sun which cannot be looked upon directly,
whoever tries will be struck down by lightning –
here is the offering of cooked manioc.
Make my child extremely strong.
Even if you have to go to the ends of the earth,
still everything belongs to you.
God, go before us; the whole earth is under your control.

Baluba, Congo   6

10 Today I bring you out of the birthing-room.
There has never been any sickness in my house;
there has never been any epidemic around my house;
there has never been any death in my house,
today I show you your child – he is also my own.
When you chop down a tree, you always try to make it
    topple.
If you hit it with an axe and don't make it fall,
it is not defeated.
May this child not be struck down by sickness in body,
or head or chest or stomach.
May he not be stricken by sickness.
You are the Lord and master of this child.
This child shows us the new way,
and his mother will bear more children.   6

Bétammaribé (Somba), Dahomey (Benin)

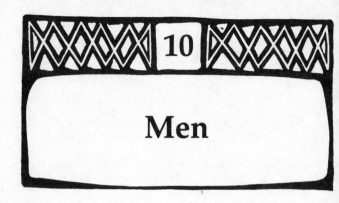

10

Men

151 God of the skies, Lord, give me strength in my life, so that I
   may be strong. Give me well-being. May I marry a wife and
   father children. May I raise goats and chickens. May I
   obtain money and all kinds of goods. May I continue to
   flourish with life and health. My daughters are daughters
   coming from God. My sons are his children. All I have is
   his. He is master of it all.

   God, Supreme Being; God, Master of the earth; you who
   have created everything, I am here before you and the
   reason why I have come here is to obtain strength in my
   life.

   May no wild beast come upon me;
   may no thunderbolt or lightning strike me;
   may no sorcerer see me;
   and may no man with evil intentions look on me.   6
   Baluba, Congo

152 CONCERNING MEDITATION

   Every man should devote much time to meditation between
   his creator and himself. He should judge himself and deter-
   mine whether his actions are correct, and whether they are
   appropriate before the Lord who has granted him life, and
   who is gracious to him every moment. If he finds that he has

acted properly, he should fear no one – no officials, no robbers, no beasts – and nothing in the universe except the Lord. When he learns this, he will have attained, first: perfection in the study of the Torah [the Law] and in meekness; and second: perfect worship wherein all material considerations are forgotten, worship which asks for no personal benefits, and which prompts one to forget his very existence.

In meditation a man may discuss his tribulations with God: he may excuse himself for his misdeeds and implore the Lord to grant him his desire to approach nearer to God. A man's offences separate him from his Maker.

Even though a man may feel he cannot concentrate adequately upon the theme of his meditation, he should nevertheless continue to express his thoughts in words. Words are like water which falls continually upon a rock until it breaks it through. In similar fashion they will break through a man's flinty heart.

In true meditation a man cries to the Lord like a child to his father who is about to go on a journey. There is no sadness in this weeping – only longing and yearning.   11

Nachman of Bratzlav

53 We know you [Ruwa,] God, Chief, Preserver,
   he who united the bush and the plain,
   you, Ruwa, Lord, Chief, the Elephant indeed,
   he who burst forth men that they lived.
   We praise you and pray to you and fall before you.
   You have sent us this animal which is of your own
      fashioning
   for you share with no man and none is given thereof.
   Chief, receive the bull of your name.
   Heal him to whom you gave it, and his children.
   Sow the seed of offspring within us,
   that we may beget like bees.
   May our clan hold together
   that it be not cleft in the land.
   May strangers not come to possess our groves.
   Now Chief, Preserver, bless all that is ours.   32

Chagga, Tanzania

154 SOLOMON'S STATEMENT OF FAITH

Like all the others, I too am a mortal man, descended from the first person made from the earth and modelled in flesh within my mother's womb. For ten months I took shape inside her, by means of man's seed and sexual pleasure, the companion of sleep. I too, when I was born, breathed in the common air; I fell on the same ground that bears us all. Like everyone else, my first sound was a baby's cry. I was nurtured in baby's clothes with every care. No king has known any different kind of existence at the beginning of life; for everyone there is one way into life, and one way out of it.

And so I prayed, and understanding was given to me; I begged, and the spirit of Wisdom came to me. I esteemed her more than the emblems of kingship and the throne of a king; compared with her, I despised riches. I did not consider any priceless stone to be her equal, for compared to Wisdom, all gold is a pinch of sand, and beside her, silver is only mud. I loved Wisdom more than health or beauty and preferred her to the light, since her radiance never sleeps. In her company all good things came to me, and at her hands riches that could not be counted. All these I delighted in, since Wisdom brings them, but as yet I did not know she was their mother. What I learned without self-interest, I pass on without reserve; I do not intend to hide her riches. For she is an inexhaustible treasure to people, and those who acquire this treasure win God's friendship, since they are commended to God by the benefits of her teaching.

The Holy Bible: Wisdom 7:1-14 (Jerusalem Bible, adapted)

155 My God, I have prayed to you: do not let me die, because I am finished in my strength even without disease. Give me food to eat now, so that I may survive. In greeting we do this: I greet you – Hail! – God, in all walks that are good. And God said: 'All right'. 29

Samburu, Kenya

156 May God grant me to speak as God alone would wish
and express thoughts worthy of God's gifts,
since God is the guide of Wisdom,
and directs the wise men.

We are indeed in God's hand, we ourselves and our
   words,
with all our understanding too, and technical knowledge.
It was God who gave me true knowledge of all that is,
who taught me the structure of the world and the
   properties of the elements,
the beginning, end and middle of the times,
the alternation of the solstices and the succession of the
   seasons,
the revolution of the year and the positions of the stars,
the nature of animals and the instincts of wild beasts,
the powers of spirits and the mental processes of human
   beings,
the varieties of plants and the medical properties of
   roots.
All that is hidden, all that is plain, I have come to know,
instructed by Wisdom who designed them all.

The Holy Bible: Wisdom 7:15-21 (Jerusalem Bible, adapted)

57 My God, give me a belt in which there are sons and in which
there are daughters. Grant me the intense yearning all
people have concerning cattle and concerning the heart.
God, agree with me.

    Do not tell untruth; do not damage other people's things,
because it is evil; because if you do, God abhors it.

    When you are travelling and see someone else's things, be
it also food that its owner had hidden, do not eat it. And if
you do eat it, notify the owner, because, if you tell him, that
is a good thing and God appreciates it. Instead, if you steal
it, it generates hatred in the hearts of everybody, and God
abhors it. God has agreed. 29

Samburu, Kenya

58 On us shall descend some awful curse, like the curse that
descended in far off times. In spite of the words of the
Creator, the people refuse to listen. On us shall descend
some awful curse, like the curse that descended in far off
times: we have but one word to say: 'Idle about! Sink in
sloth!' People of such kind will gain nothing from the
creator, the one who loves human kind. 23

Dinka, Sudan

159 God, be propitious to me!
　　Here is the New Moon:
　　keep every sickness far from me.
　　Stop the wicked one who is contemplating my
　　　　misfortune:
　　let any wicked plans fall on that person.
　　O God, be propitious to me!
　　Desert me not in my need:
　　give me children and wealth.
　　Lead to my house guests of happiness, O God!　　32

　　Duala, Cameroon

160 My God, last forever.
　　My God, grant me a girdle, multicoloured,
　　of sons and daughters.
　　My God, grant me to smell the fragrance
　　of your life that shines forever.
　　My God, we are never full of your life.
　　My God, answer to what I told you.
　　And God said: 'All right'.　　29

　　Samburu, Kenya

161 Here I am, sitting on the wall
　　waiting for a job.
　　I count the men,
　　sitting nearby
　　waiting for work.
　　Lord, can't you do something
　　so that there is more work
　　and the bosses are more just?
　　One grows lazy
　　sitting around.
　　One gets used to it.
　　And it hurts me
　　that once again
　　I can take nothing home
　　to my children and wife.
　　But I will not complain.
　　I know
　　you have everything in your hand.

And, just across the street
you let everything grow
so that at least we do not go hungry.
You are a merciful and good God.
What are these wood and clay gods
beside you?
You are the greatest,
and you do as you will.
And that is good for all.
Amen.   25

Ghana

Children

162 JACOB (ISRAEL) BLESSES JOSEPH'S SONS

May God in whose presence my fathers walked,
may God who has been my shepherd from my birth
    until today,
may the angel who has been my saviour from all harm,
bless these boys.
May my name live on in them, and the names of my
    fathers.
May they grow and increase on the earth.

The Holy Bible: Genesis 48:15-16 (Jerusalem Bible)

163 O God, turn your ear to hear me.

Protect my children and my cattle, and even if you are weary, please be patient and listen to my prayer. Under the dark cloak of night, the splendour of your world sleeps on, invisible to us. And when your sun moves across the sky each day, I continue to pray to you. May the spirits of our departed ancestors who can still exercise their influence on us, keep guard over us, from their places beyond the earth.

Nandi, Kenya 15

164 You who are deathless,
you who do not know death,

you who live always,
you who never feel the cold sleep,
your children have come to gather around you.
O Father, gird up your strength,
penetrate these young initiates with your shadow.
O Father of our race,
O Father who never dies.   23

Fang, Cameroon

65 A child is like a rare bird.
A child is precious like coral.
A child is precious like brass.
You cannot buy a child on the market.
Not for all the money in the world.
The child you can buy for money is a slave.
We may have twenty slaves,
we may have thirty labourers,
only a child brings us joy,
one's child is one's child.
The buttocks of our child are not so flat
that we should tie the beads on another child's hips.
One's child is one's child.
It may have a watery head or a square head,
one's child is one's child.
It is better to leave behind a child
than let the slaves inherit one's house.
One must not rejoice too soon over a child.
Only the one who is buried by his child
is the one who has truly borne a child.
On the day of our death, our hand cannot hold a single
    cowrie.
We need a child to inherit our belongings.   10

Yoruba, Nigeria

66 I love the Lord for he hears
my voice, my pleading.
Because he turned his ear to me
throughout my days I will call him.
Merciful is the Lord and just,
and our God has compassion.
Return, my soul, to your rest,
for the Lord has been generous to you.

What can I return to the Lord
for all his generosity to me?
I will fulfil my promises to the Lord
in the presence of all his people.
To you I offer the offering of gratitude
and call on the name of the Lord.
Praise the Lord!   11

The Holy Bible: Psalm 116

167 Hail the day on which this child is born.
    O Joy!
    Let us all sing and praise her
    that she gave birth to a son
    for whom she longed.
    Greet this day with joy.
    Our hearts are glad.   21

    Masai, Tanzania

168 O God, thanks!
    Here is the human being whom you gave us.
    Today we bring you the food that you have given us.
    You, my termite heap on which I can lean,
    from which come the termites that I eat;
    Lord, we thank you; you have given us joy
    with the numerous births you have given us.
    Nothing of all that we offer you is worthy of you.   22

    Pygmy, Zaire

169 O great [Ngewo,] God, help us, our families,
    the men of this town, the people in general,
    our pregnant women,
    our daughters and our children especially.
    May our town progress.
    May our land progress.
    May our wives not die a mysterious death
        and our men not fall from palm trees.
    Help to see that all these things do not occur.

CHILDREN

O God, help us,
and you, our ancestors,
who gave birth to us long ago,
help us so that we are well-disposed
and have good fortune,
we and our children, especially.

Mende, Sierra Leone

170 O [Muumbi,] creator,
you who have created
all human beings,
you have conferred
a great benefit on us
by bringing us this child.   20

Kamba, Kenya

171 To you, the Creator, to you, the powerful,
I offer this fresh bud,
new fruit of the ancient tree.
You are the Master; we are your children.
To you, the Creator, to you, the powerful,
[Khmvoum,] God, Khmvoum,
I offer this new plant.   23

Pygmy, Zaire

172 Hush, child of my mother,
Hush, hush O my mother!
[Imana,] God, who gave you to me,
if only I could meet him,
I would fall on my knees and pray to him,
I would pray for little babies,
for little babies on my back.

You came when the moon was shining,
you came when another was rising,
Hush, hush O child of my mother!
that we share with Imana, God,
God who gave you to me,
may he also bring you up for me.

You are ugly (or naughty) to the other Rundi,
you are beautiful (or good) to me.

Hush, child of my mother,
you came when Imana lit the fire,
you came when he was in a generous mood!
Hush, little lamb.
The lion-cub bites (he is not gentle like you).
Imana who gave you to me,
will find I have lit a fire,
and I will let him warm himself;
I found he was in a generous mood.
Hush, Imana gave you to me;
Hush, hush, I will pray to you, God,
you will give me cows and little babies.
And then you will give them increase.   33

Ruanda-Urundi, Burundi

Protection Help

73 God on high, divine King, enlighten my soul at all times. Give me, God, true faith, and perfect humility against the world's vanities. Do not give me riches, God, that may make me proud; nor poverty, that may deject me. Give me, God, some help that I may serve you, and life that I may praise you and death that I may find salvation.   11

Marrano

74 My God, guard us
in the narrow and deep valleys full of dangers,
and in the plains without end,
and in the fords we cross small or large.
And God said, 'All right!'   29

Samburu, Kenya

75 My God, place me where I may be held tightly by you. O God, let me become like a liana, like millet with very many small grains. God of the mountain of my ancestors, hear me!

May God be favourable to you: be vigorous like a tree that lasts through the annual blossoming of its shoots.

My God, grant me light for my eyes to see all things.

My God, you who are here and elsewhere, be a God who sees and hears. And God said, 'All right!'   29

Samburu, Kenya

176 I will bless the Lord at all times, and God's praise will be
continually on my lips. I will be contented in the presence of
my God. Join me in giving glory to the Lord. Let us praise
God's name together. I look for the Lord and the Lord
answers me and sets me free from all my fears. Look towards
God and be happy, and you will never be afraid.

The poor person calls out, and God hears and helps in
every trouble. God's angel camps near the one who respects
the Lord, and rescues that person. See how good God is. The
person who takes shelter in God will be happy. Respect
God, for those who do so lack nothing. Even strong lions
may go hungry and suffer, but those who look for God do
not go without blessings.

Come, my children, and listen to me, and I will teach you
true respect for God. Who wants to be fully alive; who wants
a long life and happiness? Well then, there must be no evil
on your tongue, and no wicked conversation in your mouth.
Turn away from every kind of badness and do good; look for
peace and work for peace.

God will turn away from the wicked and remove all
memories of them from the earth. God turns towards those
who are good and listens to their requests. They cry out for
help and God hears and rescues them from their suffering.
God is very close to those who are suffering in their heart.
God helps those whose spirit is sad. Even good people find
that they have many difficulties in life, but God promises to
help them to overcome their problems. God will take care of
every single bone, and not allow harm to come to you.

Wicked people will die because of their evil, and the
people who do bad things will have to pay for their wickedness; but God will come to the rescue of those who trust, and
everyone who comes to God for shelter will be safe and have
nothing to pay.

from The Holy Bible: Psalm 34

177 Now I am lying here on my mat, dear God.
The day is over and there was no work.
Still, I am tired.
And yet,
you have given us our daily bread,
and the teacher lets the children go to school without
    paying.

I don't know what they read and write there.
See to it that they learn nothing bad.
And please, if it's possible, let me find work tomorrow;
the children need something to wear.
But I am not grumbling.
Give us all a quiet night
and a sound sleep.
Protect us from the mosquitoes
and see to it that no one is cold.
Send us more ships (to Takoradi).
You are a great, powerful and loving God.
We praise you and pray to you,
Amen.   25

Ghana

78 SACRIFICIAL PRAYER

My God, grant us a life without end,
a life that goes on forever.
My God, grant us a life that proceeds in peace,
that does not end.
My God, think of us:
implored one, think of us.
My God, forgive us.
My God, great kidneys [heart] divine, do not forget us.
God of the abyss, God of the sky,
God look upon us as we invoke you.
My God, do not get annoyed, we pray you.
My God, we cling to you because of our little ones.
My God, think of us for the things we do not know.
God, free us from sins; lead us with good hearts,
and do not place us where there is evil.
God, think of new mothers: those of children and of
    animals.
God, grant us a blessed voice to invoke you night and
    morning.
God, look on us as we walk in the night and in the
    morning.
And God said: 'All right!'.   29

Samburu, Kenya

111

179 Yahweh, my God, I come before you with an open heart. I am relying on you; do not let me be ridiculed, and do not let my enemies laugh at me in scorn. Nobody who trusts in you will ever be put to shame.

Lord, show me your own ways, and teach me your paths. Point me in the direction of truth, and continue to teach me, for you are God who saves me. I trust in you all day long, Lord, because of your goodness.

Lord Yahweh, remember the goodness you always showed to me, as well as your great love. And please do not remember the sins I committed when I was young, but think of me now as I try to live according to your expectations for me.

Everyone who respects you, Yahweh God, will be taught the ways in which you want them to walk. And everyone who trusts in you will have a good life with children and some land. But we must really trust Yahweh and respect God at all times.

My eyes are always fixed on the Lord; Yahweh sets me free from nets that I am caught up in. Lord, turn to me and have pity on me. I am alone and sometimes feel very isolated and unhappy. Please set me free from my sufferings and forgive my sins.

Lord, I am asking you with full confidence to watch over and protect me. Let me not be put to shame, because I take shelter in you. Let my honesty and sincere effort be a protection for me, because all my trust is in you.

from The Holy Bible: Psalm 25

180 Lord, let your light be only for the day,
and the darkness for the night.
And let my dress, my poor humble dress
lie quietly over my chair at night.

Let the church-bells be silent,
my neighbour not ring them at night.
Let the wind not waken the children
out of their sleep at night.

Let the hen sleep on its roost, the horse in the stable
all through the night.
Remove the stone from the middle of the road
that the thief may not stumble at night.

Let heaven be quiet during the night.
Restrain the lightning, silence the thunder,
they should not frighten mothers giving birth
to their babies at night.

And me too protect against fire and water,
protect my poor roof at night.
Let my dress, my poor humble dress
lie quietly over my chair at night.   11

Nachum Bomze
Meditations before prayer (Jewish)

1 God, owner of all things, I pray thee, give me what I need
because I am suffering, and also my children are suffering,
and all the things that are in this country of mine. I beg thee
for life, the good one with possessions; healthy people with
no disease, may they bear healthy children; and also to
women who suffer because they are barren; open fully the
way by which they may see children. Give goats, cattle,
food, honey; and also, the troubles of the other lands that I
do not know, remove.   2

Meru, Kenya

2 Be with us, O God, during the coming week. Teach us to do
thy will, and make us brave in performing it. Help us to
overcome our failings, our forgetfulness of thee, our indif-
ference to the needs of others, our heedlessness of the claims
of our souls. Help us in our daily work, so that in very truth
we may live by it, making it the source of our ennoblement,
the instrument of the higher life. Help us to realise the
splendour of our religious heritage, and to fulfil more faithfully the high responsibilities it lays upon us. For so shall we
work for thy greater glory and for the establishment of thy
realm on earth. Amen.

May the will come from you
to annul wars and the shedding of blood from the
    universe,
and to extend a peace, great and wondrous, in the
    universe.
Nor again shall one people raise the sword against
    another
and they shall learn war no more.

But let the residents of earth recognise and know the
    innermost truth:
that we are not come into this world for quarrel and
    division,
nor for hate and jealousy, contrariness and bloodshed;
but we are come into this world
to recognise and know you,
may you be blessed forever.

And let your glory fill all our wits and minds, knowledge
    and hearts;
and may I be a chariot for the presence of your divinity.
May I not again depart from holiness as much as a
    hairsbreadth.
May I not think one extraneous thought.
But may I ever cling to you
until I be worthy to introduce others into the knowledge
    of the truth of your divinity.
To announce to the people your power and the honour
    of the glory of your kingdom.   11

Nachman of Bratzlav

183 PRAYER FOR THE ASSEMBLY OF THE ELDERS

May God answer us.
God, you will save us.
My God, you will guide us.
My God, think of us night and day.
Make us live long like a dark cloud – the long rains.
Make us fragrant like a citron branch that purifies.
Untie the blessed shells of mothers and of children.
God, guard us,
God, guard us,
God, guard us, and the shepherds together with us.
My God who are surrounded with stars,
with the moon at your navel,
morning of my God that will rise,
hit us with a blessed wind.
Flood us with your waters.
And God said: 'All right!'.   29

Samburu, Kenya

84 God of our ancestors, Lord of mercy, who by your words
have made everything, and in your wisdom have fitted
human beings to rule over the creatures that have come from
you, to govern the world in holiness and justice, and to carry
authority in honesty: grant me wisdom, and do not drive me
away from your family.

For I am your servant, feeble and with little time to live,
and with only a very little understanding of justice and the
laws. Indeed, if any person were perfect according to the
judgement of ordinary people, but lacking in wisdom then
that person would be nothing. You have chosen me.

Wisdom lives with you; she knows your works, and she
was present when you made the world; she understands
what pleases you and what agrees with your commandments. Send her down from heaven; send her from your
throne of glory, to help me and to work with me, and to teach
me how to please you.

Wisdom knows everything and understands everything,
and your wisdom will guide me with prudence in everything that I do. Your wisdom will protect me by her glorious
power. Then anything I do will be acceptable; I will act with
justice, and shall be worthy of my father's reward.

from The Holy Bible: Wisdom 9

85 When the foot in the night
stumbles against the obstacle that shrinks and rears and
    bites,
let, (O thou our Father, Father of our tribe,
we are thy sons,)
let it be a branch that rears and strikes,
but not one of thy sharp-toothed children,
O Father of the tribe, we are thy sons.   23

86 O God, O Master,
O Lord who knows no Lord,
O rich one who knows no poverty,
all-knowing, whose knowledge is not by learning,
king without any rival to your throne,
God of my land, my Lord,
above me, beneath me –
when misfortune strikes,

as trees protect me from the sun,
please keep far away from me this unhappiness.

O God my Lord, you sun of thirty beams.
At the approach of the enemy
do not permit me, your worm, to die on the ground.
For when we see a worm on the earth,
if we wish to, we crush him,
and if we wish, we spare him.
[Wakayo,] God,
who walk with good and evil in your hand,
my Lord, let us not be killed:
for we, your worms, have begged you!   4

Galla, Ethiopia

187   My God, grant me to walk all roads.
      My God, cover me with your cloak.
      My God, make me be covered by the black cloak
         softened by oil.
      My God, hold me tight when I walk
         and when I stand still.
      My God, do not throw me out of you.
      My God, keep me in your stomach.
      My God, guard me; God answer me.
      My God, do not throw me away.
      Listen, that we may agree on what I am telling you.
      Grant us a life that never ends,
      like the one we live.
      God, answer with favour
      to what we told you.   29

      Samburu, Kenya

188   Thou, O [Tsui-goab,] God,
      Father of our fathers,
      Thou our Father!
      Let the thundercloud stream!
      Let our flocks live!
      Let us also live, please!

I am so very weak indeed
from thirst,
from hunger!
Let me eat field fruits!
Art thou not our Father?
The Father of our fathers,
thou Tsui-goab?

O that we may praise thee!
That we may bless!
Thou Father of the fathers!
Thou our Lord!
Thou, O Tsui-goab, God!   33

Nama, South Africa

Do not reject us, O God.
Grant us to proceed peacefully, I ask you,
in all places where you have your dwelling.
Hear us.
I ask you for food for our hearts.
Do not get annoyed when we invoke you.
Only to you we turn, to reach the place
where you make us go.
Do not allow me to have difficulties with you,
because it is bad if I have difficulties.   29

Samburu, Kenya

Strong God in heaven,
I do not belong to those who
pray to you on the church hill.
Lord, I do not dare,
for my clothes are shabby;
I cannot read or write.
But I know that you are over all gods.
Lord, I know
our little idols live on our fears,
I know it,
but I fear them nevertheless.

117

Lord, you are the mighty God of heaven,
[Onyame Bekyere,] the God who provides.
Onyame Bekyere, the Christians say
that you have given us Jesus Christ.
Lord, I would like to be able to understand this.

Lord, my little idols are not
even as strong as the magician's tricks.
Those tricks are strong;
they work in the village
and a little bit along the path.
But you are lord over Kumasi and Accra,
over the ocean and over London.

Lord of Lords, I pray to you
for myself and my family,
for the palm trees from which I draw the wine.
Lord, I wish I had no fear of idols.
Strong God in heaven,
you are Lord as far as I can see –
and even farther – and here am I, skipping along
with my weak little prayer
mighty God,
what you say is coming to pass.
I cannot sacrifice much,
but your people say that
you accept even pennies.

I would love to believe in you
and not be afraid of the idols.
Please, please, please!
Amen.   26

Ghana

191 Great Spirit, piler up of rocks into towering mountains!
When you stamp on the stone, the dust rises and fills the
land. Hardness of the precipice; waters of the flood that turn
into misty rain when stirred. Vessel overflowing with oil!
Father [of Runji] who sews the heavens like cloth: let him
knit together that which is below. Caller-forth of the branching trees, you bring forth the shoots that stand erect. You
have filled the land with people; the dust rises on high, O

Lord! Wonderful one, you live in the midst of the sheltering rocks. You give rain to humankind. Hear us, O Lord! Show mercy when we beg you, O Lord! You are on high with the spirits of the great. You raise the grass-covered hills above the earth, and create the rivers, Gracious One!   33

Shona, Zimbabwe

My God, do not throw me away. God, I have invoked you. My God, be listening from your heights, and raise us up towards you. My God, be the one who is always around on the earth. Do not forget me. Help me to avoid the charge of an elephant, and may I roar like a lion.

My God, please listen, no matter how I talk to you. God, help me to last like the hump of a camel. My God, make me as solid as a mountain. God, be agreeable, so that the rain may not dry up, and that there may always be water. God, I have asked for your salvation.

God, keep me safe every morning and every evening. And at night, place me where you have placed your stars. Surround me with a blessed life. Help me to carry on in calmness, a life without stops. My God, help me to carry on with my life as a witness and a sacrifice.

My God, I have begged you; I have turned to you. My God, do not reject me, be agreeable. My God, take care of me when I go through a winding road; my God, I shall avoid a winding road – let me go along a straight road only. My God, help me to meet life; I am in danger of getting lost.

My God, I do not know what I am doing; I follow you alone, because you alone know what has to be done. You know what I shall do. My God, I have annoyed you and I stand before you now. Since the time I came, I have been begging you; God, be my God. Be the God of all.

O God, be the God of the cattle. Guard each animal as it is grazing; watch over it as it rests. My God, be watchful. Help the cattle to find grass which is still sweet. And may they drink sweet water. God, may they quench their thirst with sweet water.

O God, send the great black cloud of rain; let it not vanish like smoke. O God, be agreeable. And God said, 'All right'.

Samburu, Kenya   29

193 O God of our forebears, all our lives depend on you, and
without you we are nothing. It is you who look after wealth;
give us plenty of good harvest, rain, and wealth and children. Without you we can't live because we shall have no
food or water to drink. You are the source of life. You
protected us on our journey to this fertile land. Where we
came from, we don't know, but you know. You are the God
of wars and fights. Protect us against anyone who wants to
harm us, especially here at my home.   21

Adhola, Uganda

194 God, grant that your fruits
be our fragrance.
My God, may they not cease
to be fragrant.
My God, let your life
be my fragrance,
my God, forever, all my days.
My God, make me walk in peace;
may I walk in peace every day.
My God, I have prayed you
to grant me a long life without jolts,
like things carried by calm waters.
My God, grant that I may be like
things carried by water.
And God said, 'All right'.   29

Samburu, Kenya

195 O Father, Creator, God, I ask your help!
I invoke you, O my Father!
To you, Father, I turn,
To you, my God, I turn.
O Father, I turn to you.
God, my Father, I turn to you.
To you, in time of the new moon, I address my plea.
God recognises my ancestors who are reconciled with
    him.

Come, everyone, and beg God to give life to humankind,
come, everyone and receive life from God.
Rain mixed with sunbeams will give us life.

Ask life for the flocks, the herds, and the people.
Sacrifice the white ox, so that God may come closer,
so that the Father may give us life.

Now, let us reunite;
the Father has life to give;
the great Man has life.
O Father, Creator, come!
We are reunited.
Give life to herds, to flocks and to people.
O Father, come!
How can I reconcile myself with you?
I will invoke the Lord.   23

Dinka, Sudan

96 [Murungu,] God, we pray, help us,
that we may live and continue to have strength;
may we bear children and cattle,
and those who have them
they too say: help our children.   21

Meru, Kenya

97 My father built, and his father built,
and I have built.
Leave me to live here in success,
let me sleep in comfort, and have children.
There is food for you.   28

Banyoro, Uganda

98 Yahweh God is my rock and my deliverer. I look for safety in
Yahweh. On God I call and am saved from my enemies. In
my distress I called to Yahweh, to my God I cried; God heard
my voice, and my cry reached Yahweh's ears.
   God sends safety from on high, and hugs me tightly.
Yahweh pulls me from the deep waters and keeps me safe
from my enemies, and from enemies too strong for me.
Yahweh God was my support and set me free and rescued
me because Yahweh loves me.
   God repays me when I act justly; when my hands are pure

121

God repays me, because I have been obedient and I have not fallen away from my God. I have not disobeyed God's laws, and have kept away from sin. God, you save those who are humble.

Those who are proud, O God, you bring down to earth. But you are my lamp and you light up my darkness. With your help I can do anything. There is no God like our God. Yahweh gives me strength. Yahweh has made my enemies turn their backs on me.

Life to Yahweh God! Blessed be my rock! Let the God of my salvation be respected. For these things, I praise you, God, before the pagans, and sing the praises of your name, for ever and ever.

from The Holy Bible: 2 Samuel 22

199 My God, turn your attention to us.
I invoke you, my God, under a shady tree.
My God, look upon our group; remember your group.
My God, hear us. My God, guard our group.
My God, don't get tired; guard us; do not forget your
group.
May it be so, my God.
Put us back into our place; give us your blessings while
we are here.
My God, be the support of our group and of us who are
here,
and grant us a life of perpetual tranquillity.
God, grant to the group in this shadow, a blessed life.
May it be so, my God.   29

Samburu, Kenya

200 Friend, God, who is in this village,
as you are very great we tell you about this wound.
For you are the God of our home, in very truth.
We tell you about the fight of this lad:
let the wound heal, let it be ransomed.   8

Nuer, Sudan

201 O Sun, as you rise in the East through God's leadership,
wash away all the evils I have thought of throughout the
night.

Bless me, so that my enemies will not kill me and my
    family;
guide me through hard work.
O God, give me mercy upon our children who are
    suffering.
Bring riches today as the sun rises:
bring all fortunes to me today.   41

Luiya, Kenya

02 May you be for us a moon of joy and happiness. Let the
   young become strong and the grown man maintain his
   strength, the pregnant women be delivered and the woman
   who has given birth suckle her child. Let the stranger come
   to the end of his journey and those who remain at home
   dwell safely in their houses. Let the flocks that go to feed in
   the pastures return happily. May you be a moon of harvest
   and of calves. May you be a moon of restoration and of good
   health.   23

Mensa, Ethiopia

03 God, be a safeguard to all things.
   May God grant you the best of fragrances, so that you
       may be fragrant with life.
   May God grant you all you desire.
   May God make you reach everything that you know or
       don't know.
   My God, watch over us now.
   And God said: 'All right'.   29

Samburu, Kenya

04 You, the Great Elder, who dwells on the Kere-Nyaga,
   your blessing allows homesteads to spread.
   Your anger destroys homesteads.
   We beseech you, and in this we are in harmony with the
       spirits of our ancestors:
   we ask you to guard this homestead and let it spread.
   Let the women, the herds and flocks be plentiful.
   Chorus   Peace; praise ye [Ngai,] God. Peace be with us. 7

Kikuyu, Kenya

123

13

Reconciliation Forgiveness

205 Happy is the person whose fault is forgiven, whose sin is covered over. Happy is the person whom Yahweh God does not accuse of any guilt, and in whose spirit there is no wickedness.

I kept my sin secret, and my body was wasting away. I was groaning day after day; and by day and by night your hand lay heavily upon me, my God. My heart grew as dry as dead wood in the blazing heat.

Now at last, I have admitted to you that I had sinned. I have no longer hidden my guilt. I said: 'I will go back to Yahweh my God, and confess my fault.' And you, Lord, have forgiven my sin.

That is why every one of your children prays to you in time of trouble. And even if flood waters come rushing down, they will not reach your children. You are my hiding place, O my God.

You save me when I am in trouble and you surround me with your shouts of freedom. Many torments are waiting for wicked people, but the protection of God will enfold those who trust the Lord.

Rejoice in Yahweh God.
Be happy, good people.
Shout for joy, every upright person.

from The Holy Bible. Psalm 32

06 Ah [Ngewo,] God, you know this is my son; I begot him and
trained him and laboured for him, and now that he should
do some work for me, he refuses. In anything he now does in
the world, may he not prosper until he comes back to me and
begs my pardon . . .

Ah Ngewo, this is my son. He left me without any good
fortune in the world, because he knows I have cursed him.
He has now come back to beg me to revoke the curse, as I am
doing now. Wherever he goes now, may he prosper and
have many children.   14

Mende, Sierra Leone

07 Master of existence, and Lord of lords, we do not rely on our
own good deeds but on your great mercy as we lay our needs
before you. Lord, hear! Lord, pardon! Lord, listen and act!
What are we? What is our life? What is our love? What is our
justice? What is our success? What is our endurance? What
is our power? Lord our God, and God of our ancestors, what
can we say before you, for in your presence are not the
powerful as nothing, the famous as if they had never existed, the learned as if without knowledge, and the intelli-
gent as if without insight. To you most of our actions are
pointless and our daily life is shallow. Even the superiority
of human beings over the beasts is nothing. For everything
is trivial except the pure soul which must one day give its
account and reckoning before the judgement seat of your
glory.   11

Sabbath Morning Service (Reform Synagogues of GB)

208 You Father, and you N. . .,
why are you angry, father?
Since you left me,
I have nourished the children.
How have I wronged you?
Forgive me, father.
May the child recover.
Stand by me.   40

Nyakyusa, South Africa

209 JOB'S FINAL WORDS

I know, Yahweh God, that you are all-powerful:
whatever you think of, you can do.
I am the man who spoilt your plans
with my thoughtless and stupid words.
I have been talking about things I do not understand,
about wonders that are above me and beyond my
      knowledge.
In the past, I only knew you indirectly and by repute,
but now I have seen you and your workings, with my
      own eyes,
and I take back everything I have said without thinking.
In dust and ashes, I repent.

from The Holy Bible: Job 42: 1-6

210   Yahweh God, do not punish me in your rage, or reprove me
in the heat of anger. Now that you are angry, there is no
fitness in my flesh and no health in my bones, because of my
sin.

    My guilt is overwhelming me. It is too heavy a burden. I
am bowed down under the weight of my wrongdoing, and
every day I go about in mourning, overcome with shame.

    I feel paralysed and crushed and beaten. I moan out loud.
God, everything I need is known to you. My cries are not
secrets from you. My strength has vanished and my sight
has gone.

    My friends and my companions hide at the sight of my
wounds, and even my closest friends are now far away.
People try to kill me or threaten to ruin me, or plot to hurt
me.

    I am like a deaf person who does not hear, or a dumb
person who does not open his mouth. As if I hear nothing, I
do not make sharp replies, but I put all my trust in you,
Yahweh God.

    I have already begged you to help me. I am greatly
suffering. I admit my guilt and I am sorry for having sinned.
People are hurting me, even when I try to do good.

    Yahweh God, do not desert me. Do not stand to one side.
God, please come quickly to help me. O God, you are my
saviour.

from The Holy Bible: Psalm 38

211 May it be your will, O Lord, that no one foster hatred against us in the heart, and that we foster no hatred in our hearts against any one; that no one foster envy of us in the heart, and that we foster no envy in our hearts of any one.

Talmud   11

212 PRAYER OF THE AFRICAN NATIONAL CHURCH
USED FOR GENERAL CONFESSION

Response: May they all go away

Yahweh God, we have come before thee to worship,
and to confess our sins which we have done
during the week.   *Response*

We have sinned before thee in speaking to people,
we have offended thy creatures,
we have spoken bad words,
we have grieved their hearts, O God.   *Response*

Our Chiefs do not love one another in their hearts.
Take such hearts from them
and give them one heart.   *Response*

A new commandment you have given unto us all
to love one another as in heaven
where there is no quarrelling.
Teach us to keep thy word, O God.   *Response*

That our Chiefs may be one in loving
and ruling their country and their people,
and lead us well.
This we pray, God, grant us.   *Response*

The old worship is broken down,
we have come as wild animals
which are without God.
Call us again to worship, O God.   *Response*

Africa is the land of our ancestors.
We have changed her with our new ways,
by leaving all the ways of our ancestors,
ways which gave peace to the country, O God.   *Response*

Our Church is calling everyone to come in
so that the house of marriage may be filled.
It is thy work to give them all new dresses.   *Response*

We are taking beer as wild animals;
we forget worship which is our life.
Teach us to drink beer moderately, O God.   *Response*

We have forgotten all the laws
you gave to our ancestors.
We have married partners by snatching.
Turn us to a life of new marriages
according to the ways of our ancestors, O God.
   Response

Creator, Son and Holy Spirit,
one God ever and ever.
Amen. Amen. Amen.   39

Nyakyusa, Tanzania

213 God of our ancestors, all honour and blessing belongs to
you. May glory be given to your name forever. Your justice
can be seen in everything that you do, and you always keep
your promises faithfully. Your decisions are always fair.

In all the misfortunes that have fallen upon us, you are
completely blameless and have given us fitting punishment. Likewise, disasters have rightly fallen on our land and
towns. We deserve it; we have behaved very badly by
departing from you.

We did not listen to your laws and commandments, and
we have not done what you told us to do for our own good,
so it is fitting that we should have fallen into the hands of
enemies, and that we should be punished by disasters.

O God, please do not abandon us for ever. Do not cancel
your promises which you made long ago. Do not withdraw
your favour from us, for the sake of your friends Abraham,
Isaac and Jacob, to whom you promised descendants as
numerous as grains of sand.

Because of our sins, we are now hopeless and worthless,
and we have no way of influencing you again. So we beg
you, with sorrow in our hearts and a humbled spirit, to
accept us. There is nothing we can give you except our
sorrow.

Let our simple sacrifice today be as acceptable to you as
the greatest sacrifice possible. Help us from now on to
follow you with all our heart. From now on we are deter-
mined to follow you without reservation. Let us be received.

Do not disappoint us. Treat us gently and with mercy, because you are gentle and merciful. Let your name be given glory, O Lord. Let everyone learn that you are God and Creator, you alone. You are glorious over the whole earth.

from The Holy Bible: Daniel 3: 26-45

14 God, I have not always been true to you in my thoughts. I have doubted your goodness, your justice and your very existence. The pressures of life were too strong, its bitterness more than I could bear. Everything went wrong with my hopes and plans, and there seemed no way out, no way to turn. I said: 'There is no justice in this life of ours!' Sometimes my own suffering, but still more the suffering of others, strengthened my doubts. 'Why,' I asked, 'does God make people suffer? Where is the love? Where is the power?' At this point, you almost ceased to exist for me. Your hand would have held me, guided me, comforted me, but I lost touch with you. I should have looked for you more steadily, searched for you more diligently.

Out of my limited experience and my small knowledge, I judged the source of justice, and set my cleverness higher than the ultimate wisdom. I saw only one side of truth – the darkness, not the light. I forgot the smiling face of life and its beauty. I also forgot that the pain of life itself can lead to deeper compassion, and is a teacher of great wisdom. Because I was proud, and claimed to understand what was beyond me, I did not see that human goodness is a token of its creator's goodness.

Pardon my conceit and my blindness. Help me to greater detachment so that I may see with greater steadiness and calm. Help me to find order in the apparent chaos of human life, and love even in its defeats and trials. Your mercy is always there; you know and feel our pain. Amen.   11

Jewish

15 Have mercy on me, God, in your goodness; in your great pity and tenderness, wipe away my faults. Wash me, and wash me again, clean of all my guilt, and purify me from my sin.

I am very much aware of my faults, and my sin is constantly on my mind, because I have sinned against my God, against you alone, my God. I have done what you regard as wicked.

When you judge me guilty, you are right; when you pass sentence you are blameless. You love honesty and uprightness; teach me the secrets of wisdom. Purify me and wash me clean.

Fill me once again with joy and gladness, so that the bones you have crushed may rejoice again. Hide your face from my sins. Blot out all my guilt, O Lord.

God, make in me a new, clean heart, and put a strong and trustworthy spirit in me. Do not drive me away from you, and do not take your own holy spirit away from me.

Be the one who saves me, once again, and renew my joy; keep me steadfast and willing. I will teach those who go astray the way back to you, and sinners will return to you again.

God, my saviour, save me from death, and I will shout about your goodness. God, open my lips and my mouth will speak praises to you.

Sacrifice gives you no pleasure, and even if I were to make burnt offerings to you, you would refuse them. My broken heart is the sacrifice I bring; you will not refuse this offering.

from The Holy Bible: Psalm 51

14

Journeys and meetings

May God carry you.
Mount on God's camel that does not rock.
May God be with you, at your right and at your left.
May God lead you ahead.
Look without being seen.
May God hide you and put you into God's own secret
    place,
that you may be invisible.
Find salvation.
True is the heart of children, mothers and cattle.
Rest peacefully in the land where you shall go, a blessed
    land.
Do not bow your head in sorrow.
May God hide you from dangers
also in the open spaces without shelter.
May God place you where our creator places the stars of
    the morning.
And God said: 'All right'.   29

Samburu, Kenya

17 O grandfather, today I am going on a journey, a very long
journey. Help me on the road that I am going to take, so that I
will walk without stumbling throughout the voyage. A man
travels towards his neighbours with a joyful heart. May the

wicked man remain with his wickedness. May all unhappiness stay to one side of me, so that I may return safe and sound. And you, our God, kindly guard me and keep me safe on the road I follow. Let me walk without stumbling. May every unhappiness that you have made, be directed towards another place. Look kindly on me so that at my return, cries of joy will resound: Olo! Olo! 6

Tutshiokwé, Congo

218 RETURNING FROM A JOURNEY

O Grandfather, see, I went on a journey, and I did not see any misfortune, and I went without stumbling. Indeed you listened to my prayer, I will pay honour to you. I returned from the place to which I went, and with good things. Now you, you can take your reward. I thank you; thank you very much indeed. 6

Tutshiokwé, Congo

219 BEFORE A MEETING

My God,
who are in all things,
rise up from the abyss.
My God,
enable us to agree
both in the morning
and in the evening.
My God,
breathe upon us
with your blessed breath,
and, my God,
answer to what I have said.
And God said: 'All right'. 29

Samburu, Kenya

220   May God answer you with favour. May God support you
day and night, in the peace of the morning, and in the
afternoon, when you will be going through dangers.   29

Samburu; Kenya

221   Now you depart, and though your way may lead
through airless forests thick with *hhagar* trees,
places steeped in heat, stifling and dry,
where breath comes hard, and no fresh breeze can reach –
yet may God place a shield of coolest air
between your body and the assailant sun.

And in a random scorching flame of wind
that parches the painful throat and sears the flesh,
may God, in compassion, let you find
the great-boughed tree that will protect and shade.

On every side of you, I now would place
prayers from the holy book, to bless your path,
that ills may not descend, nor evils harm,
and you may travel in the peace of faith.

To all the blessings I bestow on you,
friend, yourself now say the last AMEN.   10

Somali, Somalia

222   May God who called our father Abraham to journey into the
unknown, and guarded him, and blessed him, may God
protect me too and bless my journey. May God's confidence
support me as I set out, may God's spirit be with me on the
way, and may God lead me back to my home in peace. Those
I love, I commend to God's care, God is with them, I shall not
fear. As for myself, may God's presence be my companion,
so that blessing comes to me, and to everyone I meet.
    Blessed are you God, your presence journeys with your
people.   11

Jewish

Marriage

223 BLESSINGS FOR THE COUPLE

May he who is supreme above all, who is blessed above all, who is great above all – may he bless the bridegroom and the bride.

Lord our God, we stand before your holiness, and in quietness thank you for bringing us to this time. May your love protect . . . and . . . who ask you to bless them. They ask your blessing not for themselves alone but for each other, and for their life together, for in your blessing is loyalty and devotion, love and trust. Be with them Lord, so that they may know true happiness and bring joy to all who love them. Let them honour you, and so bring honour to themselves. Blessed are you, who teach mankind the way to happiness.

Lord, who taught men and women to help and serve each other in marriage, and lead each other into happiness, bless this covenant of affection, these promises of truth. Protect and care for the bridegroom and bride as they go through life together. May they be loving companions, secure in their devotion which deepens with the passing years. In their respect and honour for each other may they find their peace, and in their affection and tenderness their happiness. May your presence be in their home and in their hearts.

Lord, at the quietness of this time, and in the holiness of this place, give your blessing to your children. You have given them youth with its hopes and love with its dreams. May these come true through their faith in each other and their trust in you. Let them be devoted to each other, and as the years go by, teach them how great is the joy that comes from sharing, and how deep the love that grows with giving. May your presence dwell among them in the warmth of their love, in the kindness of their home, and in their charity for others. 11

from The Marriage Service (Reform Synagogues of GB)

224 FOR A BRIDE

Meet life; meet it together with your children.
Meet it blessed, meet it near, meet it far,
the distance from south to north.
Untie your blessed shells; be a majestic tree,
refreshing to the travellers.
Spread out like palm leaves.
May God grant you children; may God grant you many
   of them,
that your food may not be sufficient.
Spread out like the water of a lake.
May you be loved by the generation now living,
and by the one that is no more.
May children call you 'grandma'.
Be an ant-hill on which children play.
Be the hinge of your door that does not fail.
May you nourish all nine generations.
Together with your axe, with numerous offspring
like a millipede's legs, go now,
for God has agreed. 29

Samburu, Kenya

225 *Blessing of the bride, Rebekah, by her sisters and father, as she went to marry Isaac*

Sister of ours, increase
to thousands and tens of thousands!
May your descendants gain possession
of the gates of their enemies!

The Holy Bible: Genesis 24: 60 (Jerusalem Bible)

226 How beautiful you are, my love, how beautiful you are!
Your eyes, behind your veil, are doves;
your hair is like a flock of goats, frisking down the
    slopes.
Your teeth are like a flock of newly washed sheep.
Each one has its twin, not one unpaired with another.
Your lips are a scarlet thread and your words enchanting.
Your cheeks, behind your veil, are halves of
    pomegranate.
Your neck is the Tower of David, built as a fortress,
hung round with a thousand shields from a thousand
    heroes.
Your two breasts are two young fawns, twins of a gazelle
    that feed among the lilies.

You are wholly beautiful, my love, and without a
    blemish.
You ravish my heart, my promised bride,
you ravish my heart with a single one of your glances.
How delicious is your love, more than good wine!
Your lips, my promised one, distil wild honey.
Honey and milk are under your tongue,
and the perfume of your clothes is wonderful.

The Holy Bible: The Song of Songs 4: 1-11 (Jerusalem Bible)

227 Start your walk towards the place where God wants you.
May God enlarge your sleeping mat; may God enlarge
    the door of your dwelling; may God enlarge your back.
May God lead you by pulling you along, and may God
    push you.
May God be at your side.
May God grant you many children.
May God grant you many cattle.
Spread out, like water of a lake. May God be your
    deliverer.
I have placed myself in front of you to lead you.

Start your walk towards the place where God wants you.
May God enlarge everything that is yours.
Be like a powerful tree, with a refreshing shadow.
Give us life.
Go without stopping.

Samburu, Kenya

29

228 How beautiful are your feet in their sandals, O Chief's
daughter!
The curve of your thighs is like the curve of a necklace,
work of a master hand.
Your navel is a bowl well-rounded, with no lack of wine,
your belly a heap of wheat surrounded with lilies.
Your two breasts are two fawns, twins of a gazelle.
Your neck is an ivory tower.
Your head is held high like the mountain, and its plaits
are dark as purple; a king is held captive in your tresses.
How beautiful are you, how charming, my love, my
delight!
In stature like the palm tree, its fruit-clusters are your
breasts.
'I will climb the palm tree', I resolved. 'I will seize its
cluster of dates'. May your breasts be clusters of grapes,
your breath sweet-scented as fruit, your speaking, great
wine.

*The Holy Bible: The Song of Songs 7: 1-10 (Jerusalem Bible,
adapted)*

229 FOR A BRIDEGROOM

I hear my beloved. See how he comes, leaping on the
mountains, bounding over the hills. My beloved is like a
gazelle or a young stag.

My beloved lifts up his voice and says to me: 'Come, then
my love, my lovely one, come. For see, the rains are over and
gone. Blossoms have appeared on the earth. The season of
glad songs has come, and the cooing of the dove is heard
over the land. The fig tree is forming its first figs. Come then
my love, my beautiful one, come.' My beloved is mine and I
am his. He pastures his flock among the lilies.

On my bed at night I sought him whom my heart loves. I
sought but did not find him. The watchmen came upon me
in the city. Scarcely had I passed him than I found him
whom my heart loves. I held him fast, nor would I let him go
till I had brought him to my mother's house. I charge you,
daughters of Jerusalem, by the gazelles, by the hinds of the
field, not to stir my love, nor rouse him, until he chooses to
awake.

*The Holy Bible: The Song of Songs 2:8 – 3:5 (Jerusalem Bible,
adapted)*

230 May God free you, may God guard you night and day.
   May God set you in your right place, and may you
      spread out like the grass of a prairie.
   Spread out like palm leaves; continue your walk,
   and may life be with you.
   May God place you where God's stars are placed
      at dawn and at night.
   Spread out like water of a lake.
   Be numerous like the feet of a millipede.   29

   Samburu, Kenya

231 Blessed are you, Lord our God, king of the universe, who
   creates the fruit of the vine.
      Blessed are you, Lord our God, king of the universe, who
   created everything for your glory.
      Blessed are you, Lord our God, king of the universe, who
   forms humankind.
      Blessed are you, Lord our God, king of the universe, who
   formed humankind in your own image, to be like you, to
   imitate you and to resemble you, and prepared from
   humankind and for humankind a constant sharing and
   renewal. Blessed are you Lord, who forms humankind.
      Let Zion, deprived of her young, rise up again and cry out
   for joy as her children are gathered around her in happiness.
   Blessed are you Lord, who gives joy to Zion through her
   children.
      Give these, companions in love, great happiness, the
   happiness of your creatures in Eden long ago. May your
   children be worthy to create a loving home, that honours
   you and honours them. Blessed are you Lord, who rejoices
   the bridegroom and the bride.
      Blessed are you, Lord our God, creator of the universe,
   who created joy and happiness, bridegroom and bride, love
   and companionship, peace and friendship. Soon, O Lord
   our God, may the sound of happiness and rejoicing be heard
   in the towns of Judah and in the streets of Jerusalem, the
   voice of the bridegroom and the voice of the bride. Blessed
   are you Lord, who causes the bridegroom to rejoice with the
   bride.

   from The Marriage Service (Reform Synagogues of GB)   11

232 My beloved is fresh and so attractive as to stand out from ten
   thousand other men. His hair is like palm leaves and as

black as a raven. His eyes are doves at a pool of water, bathed in milk, at rest on a pool. His cheeks are beds of spices, banks sweetly scented. His lips are lilies, distilling fine-smelling incense. His hands are rounded. His belly is a block of ebony. His legs are alabaster columns. His appearance is mighty, as unrivalled as the cedars. His conversation is sweetness itself; he is altogether lovable. Such is my beloved, such is my friend.

The Holy Bible: The Song of Songs 5:10-16 (Jerusalem Bible, adapted)

233 There is a season for everything, a time for every
    occupation under heaven:
A time for giving birth,
a time for dying;
a time for planting,
a time for uprooting what has been planted.
A time for killing,
a time for healing;
a time for knocking down,
a time for building.
A time for tears,
a time for laughter;
a time for mourning,
a time for dancing.
A time for throwing stones away,
a time for gathering them up;
a time for embracing,
a time to refrain from embracing.
A time for searching,
a time for losing;
a time for keeping,
a time for throwing away.
A time for tearing,
a time for sewing;
a time for keeping silent,
a time for speaking.
A time for loving,
a time for hating;
a time for war,
a time for peace.

*The Holy Bible: the Book of Ecclesiasticus 3: 1-8
(Jerusalem Bible)*

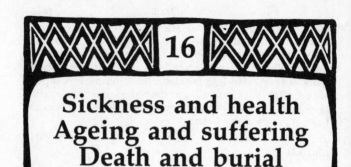

Sickness and health
Ageing and suffering
Death and burial

234 [Kirinyaga,] God, – owner of all things,
   I pray thee, give me what I need,
   because I am suffering,
   and also my children are suffering
   and all things that are in this country of mine.
   I beg thee for life,
   the good one with things,
   healthy people with no disease,
   may they bear healthy children.
   And also to women who suffer because they are barren,
   open the way by which they may see children.
   Give goats, cattle, food, honey.
   And also the troubles of the other lands
   that I do not know, remove.   32

   Meru, Kenya

235 God! give us health,
   and that it may be given to us, strength
   and that it may be given to us, milk.
   If any man eats it, may he like it.
   If the pregnant woman eats it, may she like it.   21

   Nandi, Kenya

236 God give us fatness (rain)
and we thy people shall be well;
we shall be well with health;
that is sweet.   21

Suk, Kenya

237 You Divinity, we shall kill your ox,
and better that you should be pleased with us.
You will let us walk in health,
and we have made a feast so that there should be no
    fever,
and that no other illnesses should seize people,
that they may all be well.
And if my clansman travels,
then let him complete his journey without sickness,
and let no evil befall him or anybody.
And you, Divinity, do not bring evil upon us,
and I shall be pleased.
You women, clap your hands and sing.
And *wuu* away the fever, that nothing may be wrong
    with us.
You, tribe of my father, walk in health,
nothing shall harm us,
and Divinity will be pleased with us,
and we will pray to Divinity
that there may be no bad things.
and sing . . .   32

Dinka, Sudan

238 In my sickness Lord, I turn to you, for I am your creation.
Your strength and courage are in my spirit, and your powers
of healing are within my body. May it be your will to restore
me to health.

In my illness I have learnt what is great and what is small. I
know how dependent I am upon you. My own pain and
anxiety have been my teachers. May I never forget this
precious knowledge when I am well again.

Comfort me, Lord, and shelter me in your love. Heal me
and I shall be healed, save me and I shall be saved.

Blessed are you Lord, the faithful and merciful healer.

Jewish   11

239 My God, may your answer bring us life
that proceeds calmly and surpasses the mountain-tops.
May it be a life of respite for us,
since you are a saviour who saves us all.
You save us through good fortune
in the evil we have committed.
Forgive us what we have done,
because, God, we do not know what we did,
and it was without any intention of doing evil.
We do not know what path we have walked through.
If we knew it, we would not have done it.
If it were anything obvious for all,
we would not have done it.
When we answer you, God, in a certain way,
know that it happens as I have said,
because we do not know.
My God, forgive us that evil which is unintentional.
Let it be so, my God.
Restore all our hearts, so that
we may follow your goodness.
By means of your strength remove from us
the evil that is within our hearts.
God, answer!
Yes! God has answered.   29

Samburu, Kenya

240 Slowly the muddy pool becomes a river
slowly my mother's disease becomes death.
When wood breaks, it can be repaired.
But ivory breaks for ever.
An egg falls to reveal a messy secret.
My mother went and carried her secret along.
She has gone far –
we look for her in vain.
But when you see the Kob antelope on the way to the
    farm,
when you see the Kob antelope on the way to the river –
leave your arrows in the quiver,
and let the dead depart in peace.   9

Yoruba, Nigeria

41 Out of the depths I cry out to you, O Lord,
  Lord, hear my voice!
  O let your ears be attentive
  to the voice of my pleading.

  If you, O Lord, should mark our guilt,
  Lord, who would survive?
  But with you is found forgiveness:
  for this we respect you.

  My soul is waiting for the Lord,
  I count on his word.
  My soul is longing for the Lord
  more than watchman for daybreak.

  Let the watchman count on daybreak
  and Israel on the Lord.

  Because with the Lord there is mercy
  and fulness of redemption.
  Israel indeed he will redeem
  from all its iniquity.

  The Holy Bible: Psalm 130 (Grail version)

42 My God, do not take away anything else from us;
  my God, leave to us the good of our bodies.
  My God, make us overflow with life;
  my God, give us a life of prosperity;
  make us prosper on earth, my God.
  God, grant us continuity,
  to prosper in all things
  and in all you give us.
  My God, listen to what I told you.
  And God said: 'All right'.   29

  Samburu, Kenya

43 God, Supreme Being,
  here I am, very unhappy,
  for all my possessions are scattered at random.
  My family and my heart are completely overturned.
  I who have never committed theft,
  who have never bewitched anyone,
  my possessions here are the property of all my family;

143

they are the things inherited from my ancestors.
All people have goods which coexist with them in peace;
but my house is as if consumed by fire.
My God, you arrange all the affairs of men and women;
I have kept all the rules and taboos;
I have offered chickens,
I have called upon the ancestors,
everything is useless.
Now it's up to you, God,
why not strike down the person
who has a grudge against me?
My goods and my neighbours, all of us
belong to you, God.
You, Sun that we are unable to look at directly,
you, life force, worshipped by our lineage heads,
my misery overflows.
I, who never seduced the wife of another man,
who have never taken another man's goods by force,
who has no charm to harm anyone else,
who is jealous of no one; I am ruined.
Everyone else has possessions which prosper;
my own possessions evaporate on all sides,
and are always getting lost.
God, Supreme Being, Sun that we cannot look upon
    directly,
I am running headlong to my ruin, with all that I have.
Even sleep deserts me in my own house.
May the person who bears me a grudge suffer
    misfortune!
May the one emboldened to shout: 'I wish nothing good
    to this man;
I have made a powerful fetish to work against him',
    may that one be jeered at and mocked in public.   6

Baluba, Congo

!44 My God, my God, why have you deserted me? You are so far
     away from my cries of distress. My God, I cry out to you all
     day long but you never seem to answer. I am begging your
     help at night, but I cannot find peace or rest.
        O God, our ancestors put their trust in you and you
     rescued them. They shouted out to you for help and they

were saved. When they called to you, they escaped. But I am a worm and not a man, scorned by the people. Everyone who sees me jeers; people sneer at me.

'He relied on Yahweh God', they say. Let Yahweh save him. If God is his friend, let him save him. Yes, it was you, God, who took me from the womb and entrusted me to my mother's breasts. I was promised to you from my birth.

From my mother's womb you have been my God. Do not leave me alone in my suffering. Come close for there is no one else to help. I am like water draining away, and my bones are all dislocated. My heart is melting like wax and my mouth is drier than burnt clay.

My tongue is stuck to the roof of my mouth and a pack of dogs surrounds me. Wicked men are closing in on me, and they are tying me hand and foot. They leave me lying in the dust of death. I am so thin I can count every one of my bones.

My enemies stare at me and mock me. They steal my clothes and share them among themselves. O Lord, do not leave me alone. You are my only strength; hurry to help me! Rescue my life from the grip of these dogs and save me from these wild beasts.

I will tell of your great name to my brothers, and will praise you before all the people. 'You who respect God, praise him!' For he has never despised or looked down on the poor man in his poverty; he has not hidden, but has heard the poor man's cries.

O God, you I will praise in public. I will perform my vows before those who respect God. The poor will receive as much as they can eat. Those who look for Yahweh God will praise him. May their hearts remain strong for ever and ever.

The whole earth, from one end to the other, will remember and return to the Lord. All nations will worship him. God reigns, forever and ever, and all the wealthy people of the earth will bow down before him; indeed, everyone on the earth will bow before him.

My whole life will be dedicated to Yahweh God and my children shall serve him. They shall tell of the Lord to generations yet unborn, and they shall proclaim his faithfulness to people yet to come: 'These things the Lord has done', they will say.

from The Holy Bible: Psalm 22

245 Let us behave gently,
    that we may die peacefully;
    That our children may stretch out their hands
    upon us in burial.   16

    Yoruba, Nigeria

246 Happy is the man who takes care of the poor and the weak; if
disaster strikes, Yahweh will come to help him. God will
guard him and give him life and happiness. Do not let his
enemies treat him as they please. God will be his comfort on
his bed of sickness.

    I myself said: 'Yahweh God, have pity on me! Cure me, for
I have sinned against you'. My enemies speak of me with
evil hearts: 'How long before he dies and his name dies with
him?' They come to visit me, with spiteful hearts. They do
not bring me any comfort at all, but spread news of my
misfortune with glee.

    All the people who hate me whisper to each other about
me. They agree that I deserve the misery I suffer. They say:
'His sickness will lead to his death; he is beaten now; he will
never recover.' Even my closest and most trusted friend who
used to share my food, has turned away from me.

    But you, Yahweh, take pity on me! Raise me up to good
health, and I will show these enemies of mine that I enjoy
your favour. Let it happen that I will be unharmed because
of your protection. I will remain in your presence forever.
Blessed be Yahweh God, forever and for all eternity, Amen.
Amen.

    from The Holy Bible: Psalm 41

247 You, [Father,] God,
    who are in the heavens and below;
    creator of everything and understanding everything;
    maker of the earth and of the heaven –
    we are but little children
    unknowing anything evil.
    If this sickness has been brought by a person
    we beg you, help us through these roots.
    In case it was inflicted by you, the Conserver,
    likewise we beg your mercy on your child.

Also you, our grandparents, who sleep in the place of the
    shades,
we beg all of you who sleep on one side:
all ancestors, males and females, great and small,
help us in this trouble, have compassion on us,
so that we can sleep peacefully.
And so I spit out this mouthful of water!
Pu-pu! Pu-pu!
Please listen to our earnest request.   21

Luguru, Tanzania

48 My God, do not take away from me this fresh water.
  My God, grant me to quench my thirst again with this
      water.
  My God, morning of my God, who are rising,
  rise over us in peace.
  God of the mountain of our fathers,
  God of the mountain of reeds,
  my God, I have prayed to you.
  Do not come with bad things.
  My God, grant me to proceed tranquilly,
  as long as I hold the staff of my authority.
  My God, allow me to reach an old age without end,
  and grant that I might be covered by you and my
      children
  with blessed leaves.
  And may I be buried by the children of my son,
  and may they call me grandfather (grandmother).
  When I die, do not allow any children to be distressed.
  When I am dying, my son, do not allow a beast to eat
      me.
  When I fall asleep forever, let me lie down in the best
  way so that God may help you.
  Never show evil to God.
  When I die, place me in a grave:
  dig a deep grave within the cattle enclosure:
  bury me within the enclosure of our cattle.
  If you do so, God will help you;
  truly so, my son.   29

  Samburu, Kenya

249 The promise that you promised, you, God of my father,
where is it? You trees, hear my words; and you grass, hear
my words; and you, God, hear my words, and you earth,
hear my words . . . O Divine one, because of sickness, you
will help out my tongue. For we have dedicated the ox and
invoked over it. And if a person has his sickness as a result
of malice, then that person will find what he deserves. 21

Dinka, Sudan

250 That we may not die young;
that we may not attain an old age of wretchedness;
that we may not scratch the ground with a stick
in the place of sacrifices. 32

Yoruba, Nigeria

251 Listen to me, Yahweh God, and answer me,
for I am poor and needy.
Preserve my life, for I am devoted to you;
save the servant who trusts in you.

You are my God; have mercy on me, Lord,
for I cry out to you all day long.
Give your servant some cause for rejoicing,
for to you, Lord, I offer my life.

Lord, you are good and you forgive;
you are full of love to all who call on you.
Pay attention, Lord, to my prayer,
and listen to me as I beg you.

In days of trouble, I call out to you
and surely you will reply.
There is no God to compare with you,
and no achievement to compare with yours.

All the pagans will come to worship you, Lord,
and they will give glory to your name;
for you are great and you do marvellous things,
you alone are God.

O God, show me your way, and
how I should walk faithfully beside you.
Make me single-hearted in respecting your name.

SICKNESS AND HEALTH

I thank you with all my heart, O God,
and I give glory to your name forever,
for your love to me has been so great,
you have rescued me from the depths of the grave.

Proud ones have risen up against me;
brutal ones are hounding me to death:
they are people to whom you mean nothing.

Lord God, you who are always merciful and tender-
    hearted,
slow to anger, always loving, always loyal,
turn and have pity on me.

Give me your strength, your saving help;
I am your servant, the child of a sincere mother.
Yahweh God, give me proof of your goodness.

from The Holy Bible: Psalm 86

2 Blessed are you Lord, my God, spirit of the universe, who
brought me across the bridge of life. When the dim light of
my own self will sink and merge within the light which
illumines the world and eternity, I shall conclude the order
of my days.
    In this twilight flow of my life, I stand before the dawn of
my new sun with tense consciousness, about to die and to
live, a being who feels at one with the universe and eternity,
as in the ancient words: 'Hear, Israel, the Lord our God, the
Lord is One.' Blessed is the God of life and death, of light
and love.   11

3 O God, thou art great,
    thou art the one who created me,
    I have no other.
    God, thou art in the heavens,
    thou art the only one:
    now my child is sick,
    and thou wilt grant me my desire.   30

Anuak, Sudan

149

254 God, agree with us; wake up.
God, watch; my God be my relief.
May God relieve me of this disease of mine.
God, give me your medicine,
your blessed medicine that does not die or end,
for a good life.
Grant a lasting life that may not run away while we live.
Grant a life that does not stop.
Grant a strong heart;
grant what comes on a blessed night,
that we may always find it while we live.
Grant a blessed voice that may be heard continually,
like a blessed bell.
Listen to it when you sleep and when you walk.
May God grant you a strong horn that does not break,
that lasts forever.   29

Samburu, Kenya

255 [Nyaga,] Brightness, help this man that he may be well,
that he may recover tomorrow,
and may you want to help this man to be well;
and, as overcoming you overcame,
overcome all these troubles,
and have mercy on me,
because we do not know how to pray to God
differently from what we say now.   32

Meru, Kenya

256 O Lord, I take shelter in you;
let me never be shamed.
In your justice, rescue me and set me free,
listen to me and save me.

Be a rock and shelter me,
be a fortified dwelling to protect me!
You are my rock and my stronghold;
set me free from wicked people.

You alone are my hope, Lord.
I have put my trust in you since I was young.
You have been my strength since I was in my mother's
    womb.
My hope and trust have always been in you.

Many people are puzzled when they see me,
but I have always relied on you above all.
Praises of you are always on my lips,
and I give you glory all day long.

Now that I am old, do not reject me;
do not leave me now that my strength is failing,
for my enemies are talking about me
and people are planning to hurt me.

They say:God has deserted this one, follow him
and seize hold of him; there is no one to save him.
God, do not leave me!
My God, come quickly and help me.

I will never give up hope; I will praise you always.
All day, every day, I will speak of your justice.
I will tell of your power to save.
You have taught me this since my youth.

Now that I am old and grey-haired,
do not desert me, O God.
Let me live to tell the young about your power.
I will tell them about your great goodness.

You have sent me hardships and difficulties,
but you will give me life again.
I know you will support me from the depths,
you will lift me up and console me.

So I will thank you in music
for your faithful love, my God.
I will sing and play music to you,
O Holy God!

My mouth shall sing your praises as I play to you,
and my soul, redeemed, will sing for joy.
All day long I shall speak about your justice.
May shame and disgrace fall on those who plot evil.

The Holy Bible: Psalm 71 (Jerusalem Bible, adapted)

257 May we be in good health always;
   remove all misfortunes from us.
   May sickness be gone;
   may poverty be gone;
   may death be gone;
   instead, may abundant life be ours forever.
   Provide the necessary protection for all members of the
      lineage,
   in the same way as they have all gathered to honour you
      today.
   May all members of the public be kind to us.
   Give us success when we go to farm;
   give us success when we go to fish;
   give us success when we go to trade.
   O venerable one, abundant life and prosperity for all of
      us.   12

   Anlo Ewe, Ghana

258 I am happy, O God, at what you have done.
   The righteous shall flourish like the palm tree,
   grow tall like a cedar in Lebanon.
   Planted in the house of the Lord
   they shall flourish in the courts of our God,
   bearing new fruit in old age
   still full of sap and still green,
   to declare that the Lord is upright,
   my rock in whom there is no wrong.   11

   from The Holy Bible: Psalm 92

259 Father, thank you for your revelation
         about death
         and illness
         and sorrow

   Thank you for speaking so plainly to us,
      for calling us all friends
      and hovering over us;
      for extending your arms out to us.

   We cannot stand on our own;
      we fall into death without you.
      We fall from faith, left to our own.
      We are really friendless without you.

Your extended arms fill us with joy,
   expressing love,
   love caring and carrying,
   asking and receiving our trust.

You have our trust, Father,
   and our faith,
   with our bodies
   and all that we are and possess.

We fear nothing when with you,
   safe to stretch out and help others,
   those troubled in faith,
   those troubled in body.

Father, help us to do with our bodies what we proclaim,
   that our faith be known to you
   and to others,
   and be effective in all the world.   27

Masai, Tanzania

60 God has answered
to the words we told him,
and we have answered
to God's words,
so that when we die
God may put us in a good place,
as we do not know (what happens)
when one dies.
So, we pray to God
every day.
Keep away from unjust curses,
because we do not know
God's words,
because
God loves
a good speech,
and because God
is pleased
if we walk
along a good road.   29

Samburu, Kenya

261 PRAYERS ON BEHALF OF THE SICK

Lord, I pray for .... who is sick and in pain. May it be your will to renew his/her strength and bring him/her back to health. Renew his/her spirit also and free him from anxiety for you watch over his/her body and his/her soul.

Though I cannot share his/her pain, help me to bring him/her good cheer and comfort. Give us the joy of helping each other through all the fortunes of life.

Blessed are you Lord, the faithful and merciful healer.   11

Reform Synagogues of GB

262 DURING DANGEROUS ILLNESS

As a child turns to his father, I turn to you, my God who created me. You are the master of my life and death, may it be your will to heal me and keep me in life. But if it is time for me to go forward, through death to life everlasting, give me courage and trust to ease my journey.

Forgive my sins, and my soul will be pure as it returns to you. Protect those I love whom I leave behind, for their lives are in your care. Through your mercy we shall come together in the gathering of life. In your hand I lay my soul, when I sleep and when I wake, and with my soul my body too. You are with me, I shall not fear.   11

Reform Synagogues of GB

263 ON BEHALF OF THE DANGEROUSLY ILL

I pray to you for my beloved .... who approaches the frontiers of this life. You, God, are the controller of life, and death and his/her fate is in your hands. Heal his/her body and restore him/her to me, if this is your will. If it is not be with him/her where I cannot follow, and give him/her courage to conquer pain, and hope to overcome fear. Lead him/her forwards in peace from this world into the life that has no end, supported by his/her own good deeds, and accompanied by my love. Help me too, and teach me that though we may part now, we shall come together once again in the gathering of life. His/her soul is in your hand, and with his/her soul, his/her body too. You are with him/her, I shall not fear.   11

Reform Synagogues of GB

Merciful Father, be with us as we gather in this house, the home of our dear one who has gone forward to life everlasting. We remember all his/her goodness. May his/her memory be a blessing.

Help us to remember that the soul does not die, and our dear one has gone to that eternal home which you prepared for us when our work on earth is done, and our time here has ended. Open the gates of mercy for him/her. May he/she enter into everlasting peace. In your light we see beyond the frontiers of death to the life that has no end.

This house was built by human hands, but we shall come together in a home where we shall never part, surrounded by your presence. Amen.

MEMORIAL SERVICE

The souls of the righteous are in the hands of God, and no harm shall touch them. In the eyes of the ignorant they appeared to die, and their going seemed to be their hurt. But they are at peace, and their hope is full of immortality. Their chastening was slight compared to the great good they shall receive. God has put them to the test and proved them worthy to be with God.

Wisdom of Solomon 3: 1-5

Lord God, source of all being and fountain of life, what can we say to you, for you see and know all things. In your wisdom you formed the universe and in your love you provided for all your creatures. What can we do, but acknowledge your power, accept your gifts with gratitude, and according to your will, give you back your own.

Lord God, may the light of your presence shine on us as we gather here, our hearts bowed down by the loss of .... whom you have gathered to yourself. Accept in your great mercy the earthly life which has now ended and shelter with your tender care this soul that is so precious to our hearts.

We thank you for all that was gentle and noble in his/her life. Through his/her name inspire us with strength and light. Help us to use our grief itself for acts of service and of love.

Everlasting God, help us to realise more and more that time and space are not the measure of all things. Though our eyes do not see, teach us to understand that the soul of our dear one is not cut off. Love does not die, and truth is stronger than the grave. Just as our affection and the memory of the good he/she did unite us with him/her at this time, so may our trust in you lift us to the vision of the life that knows no death.

God of our strength, in our weakness help us; in our sorrow comfort us; in our confusion guide us. Without you our lives are nothing; with you there is fulness of life for evermore.

May the words of my mouth and the meditation of my heart be acceptable to you, O Lord, my rock and my redeemer.   11

Reform Synagogues of GB

265 As for me, [Imana,] God, has devoured me.
As for me God has not dealt with me as with others.
With singing I would sing
if only my dead brother were with me.
Sorrow is not to hang the head in mourning,
sorrow is not to go weeping – to weep will not remove
    sorrow.
As for me, Imana has devoured me.
As for me God has not dealt with me as with others;
if Imana had dealt with me as with others
I could be the 'scorner-of-enemies'.
Woe is me!   38

Rwanda-Urundi, Burundi

Night prayers

266 God, save us.
God, hide us.
When we sleep, God do not sleep.
If we sleep, God do not get drowsy.
Tie us around your arm, God,
like a bracelet.
Guard us now, my God, guard us and save us.
God, guard for us our little ones
both people and beasts,
whether awake or asleep.
God, look on us with a countenance that is happy.
Hit us with the black cloud of rain like the long rains.
God, give us your waters.
God, give us what we ardently desire in regards to
   children,
and to cattle.
God, do not make our land barren.
God, give us places where there is life.
God, divide us fairly into dead and alive.
And God said: 'All right'.   29

Samburu, Kenya

267 Lord, may I sleep in peace and wake up to a good life. Cover
me with the shelter of your peace and protect me because
you are good.

The Lord will guard your going out and your coming in,
now and for evermore.

HEAR O ISRAEL, THE LORD IS OUR GOD, THE LORD
IS ONE. LOVE THE LORD YOUR GOD WITH ALL YOUR
HEART, AND ALL YOUR SOUL, AND ALL YOUR MIGHT.

> Within God's hand I lay my soul
> both when I sleep and when I wake,
> and with my soul my body too,
> my Lord is close, I shall not fear.

Blessed be the Lord by day; blessed be the Lord by night.
Blessed be the Lord when we lie down; blessed be the Lord
when we rise up.   11

Evening Prayers (Reform Synagogues of GB)

268 Lord, listen to my prayer and pay attention when I beg.
Answer me, because you are faithful and just.
Do not put me on trial, because no one is virtuous before
    you.

The enemy is chasing me, to crush my life in the dust.
He forces me to live in darkness like the dead, forgotten.
My strength fails and my heart is full of fear.

I remember the days that are past.
I reflect on all that you have done, and I stretch out my
    hands.
Like earth without water, so my soul is thirsty for you.

Lord, hurry and answer before I become too weak.
Do not hide your face, or I will be like a dead body.
In the morning, let me know for sure of your love.

I put all my trust in you.
Show me the path that I should follow.
Lord, rescue me from my enemies.

I have run to you for protection.
Teach me to obey you, since you are my God.
Let your spirit be my guide on to level ground.

Lord God, be true to your name of Saving One.
Show me your love and protect me from oppression.
In your goodness save me from worry and fear.

from The Holy Bible: Psalm 143

269 If you live in the shelter of the Most High
and make your home in the shadow of the Almighty,
you can say to Yahweh God: 'My safety, my defence,
my God in whom I trust!'

God will set you free from the traps
set by hunters trying to destroy you.
You need not fear the terrors of the night.

You need not fear the plague that prowls in the dark.
A thousand may fall at your right hand side
but you will remain safe.

No disaster will overtake you,
and no sickness will come near your dwelling place,
for God's angels will guard and support you.

They will support you in case you trip on a stone.
You will tread on deadly snakes or wild animals
and you will not be injured.

I, the Lord, rescue everyone who relies on me.
I protect those who call on my name.
I answer whoever cries out to me in trouble.

If you call I will say: 'I am with you'.
I will give safety and honour.
I will let you see my saving power.

from The Holy Bible: Psalm 91

270 My God, turn your thoughts to us;
do not reject us.
Stars of my God, moon of my God,
be our support.
Grant us nourishment.
Be our support.
Grant us life in cattle and children.
God, grant us what is desired.
Horn-of-my-buffalo, be our support.
White fleece of all riches,
my breast, grant us what is desired,
and grant us what does not end.
My God, founder of my family,
my creator who are in the skies,
be our support.

My God, do not reject me,
because I shall not reject you.
Remember me when I sleep and when I walk.
My God, give me rain.
Turn your thoughts to our children.
Turn your thoughts to our cattle.
My God, be my support.   29

Samburu, Kenya

271 O God, you have let me pass this day in peace,
    let me pass the night in peace
    O Lord who has no Lord,
    there is no strength but in thee.
    Thou alone hast no obligation.
    Under thy hand I pass the night.
    Thou art my mother and my father.   36, 31

    Boran, Kenya

272 When I call, you answer me, O God of justice,
    When I am in trouble you come to release me,
    Now be good to me and hear my prayer.

    O people, how long will your hearts be closed?
    How long will you love what is futile and seek for what
        is false?
    Be sure that Yahweh works wonders for all God's loved
        ones.

    Yahweh God hears me when I call.
    Tremble; give up sinning.
    Spend your night in quiet meditations and be still.

    Make justice your sacrifice, and trust in the Lord.
    Many people say: what can bring us happiness?
    O Lord, lift up the light of your face on us.

    Yahweh God, you have put more joy into my heart
    than others ever knew, for all their corn and new wine.
    I will lie down in peace and fall asleep at once,
    since you alone, Yahweh God, make me rest in safety.

    from The Holy Bible: Psalm 4

273 Lord God, grant that we might sleep in peace
in this hut;
and that at the break of day
we may find ourselves in safety.   35

   Diola, Cameroon

274 Now that evening has fallen,
to God the Creator will I turn in prayer,
knowing that God will help me.
I know the Creator will help me.   23

   Dinka, Sudan

275 Hear O Israel, the Lord is our God, the Lord is One.
   Blessed is the name of God, whose glorious kingdom is
forever and ever.
   Love the Lord your God with all your heart, and all your
soul, and all your might. These words that I command you
today shall be upon your heart. Repeat them to your children, and talk about them when you sit in your home, and
when you walk in the street; when you lie down, and when
you rise up. Hold fast to them as a sign upon your hand, and
let them be as reminders before your eyes. Write them on
the doorposts of your home and at your gates.

   The Holy Bible: Deuteronomy 6: 4-9

276 God, be watchful; watch over us now.
My God, answer favourably what I ask you.
Do not get tired, but keep awake and watch over us.
Pasture all creatures everywhere.
Do not rest; provide a shepherd of the night and of the
   day.
Do not throw us away; support us by our armpits.
Watch over us and look upon us a lot.

Provide stars continually for the night and for the day.
Place us where the stars are.
Move around with your blessed swarm – the Milky Way –
where our cows are, and our goats and sheep.
Be watchful where mothers are, and elders.
Place fertility (the placenta) where our young brides are
and our cows and our sheep.

161

My God, do not do any evil to us.
My God, guard our shepherds.
Guard our cattle.
Guard and watch over those who can see and those who
    do not have eyes,
because they are all poor:
the one who has eyesight is also poor:
both the one who has and the one who has not – watch
    over them all.

God, watch over everybody,
over those who live and those who don't.
Watch over all, over children who are born
and over those who are not born,
and over those still in the womb.
God, watch over all of them,
and over all others too.

Protect everybody who is here, and those who are not.
God, guard our children,
those who are far or near.
Watch over far places and near ones.
Guide all our children, that they may get home.
My God, watch over and protect
all our children and all our lands.

My God, give us life year after year,
that I may master life,
that I may master a long life
and advance into old age.
May God grant (you) what is desired,
and (your) daily food.
And God said: 'All right'.   29

Samburu, Kenya

277 I implore thee, God,
    I pray to thee during the night.
    How are all people kept by thee all days?
    And thou walkest in the midst of the grass,
    I walk with thee;
    when I sleep in the house I sleep with thee.
    To thee I pray for food, and thou givest it to the people
    and water to drink.   37

    Shilluk, Sudan

278 Come, Lord,
 and cover me with the night.
 Spread your grace over us
 as you assured us you would do.

 Your promises are more than
 all the stars in the sky;
 your mercy is deeper than the night.
 Lord, it will be cold.
 The night comes with its breath of death.
 Night comes; the end comes; you come.

 Lord, we wait for you
 day and night.   26

 Ghana

279 Let us not run the world hastily;
 let us not grasp at the rope of wealth impatiently;
 what should be treated with mature judgement
 let us not treat in a fit of temper.
 Whenever we arrive at a cool place
 let us rest sufficiently well.
 Let us give prolonged attention to the future,
 and then let us give due regard to
 the consequences of things,
 and that is on account of our sleeping.   16

 Yoruba, Nigeria

280 [Ngai,] Lord, you are the Lord, help me sleep well,
 so that I may get up tomorrow
 with my limbs healthy;
 and show me the work I have to do.   32

 Meru, Kenya

281 I trust in you Lord; deliver me;
   my life is in your hands;
 through your love, save me.
 Into your hands O Lord, I commend my spirit.

 Look at me; answer me, Lord my God;
   open my eyes
 that I may not sleep in death.
 Into your hands, O Lord, I commend my spirit.

Guard me like the pupil of your eye;
   hide me
in the shadow of your wings.
Into your hands, O Lord, I commend my spirit.

I lie down and sleep in peace;
   you alone, Lord,
keep me safe.
Into your hands, O Lord, I commend my spirit.

In joy I will look upon your face, Lord;
   when I awake
I will be satisfied with your face.
Into your hands, O Lord, I commend my spirit.   5

The Holy Bible: Psalms

282 God, think of us. Give us your breath that is blessed.
My God, encircle us with your life in our children
and our cattle, day and night.
Blessed swarm of God, make us enjoy your fragrance.
God, I have wanted to talk to you, so
answer me with your favour.
And God said: 'All right'.   29

Samburu, Kenya

283 Master of all the worlds, fountainhead of all
   happiness . . .
Help me to immerse my meditations and all the impulses
   of my heart and the depths of my thought in the
   mysteries of joy . . .
And grant, O my Creator,
that I believe with complete faith that all fires of
   suffering
and all the nine measures of destitution and illness and
   pain, and the heaps of trouble in this world, and
   punishment in the next world, and
all the deaths –
that they are as nothing:
as absolutely nothing
as absolutely nothing
against the wondrous joy of clinging to your godliness.
Therefore does my prayer stretch itself before you.

164

My Father in heaven,
save me and help me from this moment to be alone in
  the fields every night . . .
to cry out to you from the depths of my heart . . .
to set forth all the burdens and negations that remove
  me from you,
Light of Life,
and give strength to strengthen myself in spite of
  everything –
to strengthen myself with great happiness,
with happiness that has no end,
until my heart lifts up my hands to clap, to clap, to clap,
  and my legs to dance until the soul swoons, swoons.
And help me ever to make a new beginning and to be a
  flowering well of prayer,
to work always with quickened spirit,
and to stand with powerful strength against the scoffers
  and mockers,
who go about in our days – days of double darkness . . .
but oh, against all the trouble and burdens,
your joys and your delights are strong and powerful . . .
oh our great Father, home of delights and wellspring of
  joy.   11

Nachman of Bratzlav

284 Come now, all of us who bless The Lord God, let us bless
    Yahweh now. And let us renew our dedication to serve God
    in worship and in living every day of our lives. Let us stretch
    out our hands as a sign of blessing and agreement, in the
    direction of the place where we come to worship God, and
    let us bless God's name night after night. May the great
    blessings of Yahweh God, come down upon us all and
    remain with us always. Yahweh made the earth and the
    whole of creation. Let us bless God's name night after night.

from The Holy Bible: Psalm 134

General intercessions

285 *The following may be used as intercessions. Each one may be concluded with a response:*

Leader: Lord in your mercy
All: Hear our prayer.
or
Leader: Lord hear us.
All: Lord graciously hear us.
or
Leader: For this let us pray to the Lord.
All: Lord, hear our prayers.

You favour humankind with knowledge, and teach mortals understanding. Favour us with the knowledge, understanding and discernment that come from you.

Turn us back to your teaching, our Maker, and draw us near to your service, our Ruler. Bring us back in perfect repentance to your presence.

Forgive us, our Creator, for we have sinned; pardon us, our Ruler, for we have disobeyed; for you are a God who is good and forgiving.

Look upon our affliction and defend our cause, and rescue us quickly for the sake of your name. For you are a mighty redeemer.

Heal us, Lord, and we shall be healed; save us, and we shall be saved; for it is you we praise. Send relief and healing for all our diseases, our sufferings and our wounds; for you are a merciful and faithful healer.

Bless this year, O Lord our God, and may all that it brings be good for us; send your blessings over the face of the earth, satisfy us with your goodness, and make our years good years.

Sound the great horn for our freedom, and speedily may the voice of liberty be heard in the cities of our lands, for you are a God who redeems and rescues.

Restore your judgment of righteousness in the world. Turn away from us sorrow and pain, rule over us with love and mercy, and judge us with righteousness.

Fulfil in our time the words of your servant David, so that we are again ruled in justice and in the fear of God. Let light dawn in the world in our days, for we wait and work for your salvation.

Hear our voice, Lord our God, father of mercy. Spare us and have pity on us, and receive our prayer with love and favour. For you are a God who listens to our prayers and needs. Our king, do not turn us away empty from your presence, for you hear the prayers of all lips.   11

from Daily Amidah (Reform Synagogues of GB)

Bibliography*

1 Agunwa, C., *More than Once*, London 1967, 107
2 Bernardi, B., *The Mugwe, A Failing Prophet*, Oxford 1959 181
3 Brown, J.T., *Among the Bantu Nomads*, Seeley, Service & Co, London 1926 100
4 Buhlmann, W., *The Chosen Peoples*, St Paul 1982 31, 186
5 Deiss, Lucien, *Come, Lord Jesus*, World Library, Chicago 1982 22, 281
6 Dieterlen, G., (ed) *Textes sacrés d'Afrique Noire*, Gallimard 1965 36, 65, 72, 80, 147, 149, 150, 151, 217, 218, 243
7 Donovan, V., *Christianity Rediscovered*, S C M 1978 13
8 Evans-Pritchard, E., *Nuer Religion*, Oxford 1956 96, 200
9 Finnegan, R., *Oral Literature in Africa*, Oxford 1970 240
10 Finnegan, R., (ed) *The Penguin Book of Oral Poetry*, Allen Lane 1978 9, 49, 105, 165, 220
11 *Forms of Prayer, Daily and Sabbath*, 1977. Edited by the assembly of Rabbis of the Reform Synagogues of Great Britain 6, 20, 26, 28, 30, 32, 33, 34, 40, 47, 48, 50, 54, 56, 57, 61, 62, 63, 83, 87, 88, 90, 97, 109, 110, 111, 115, 117, 118, 125, 126, 127, 132, 133, 134, 140, 141, 148, 152, 173, 180, 182, 207, 211, 214, 222, 223, 231, 238, 252, 258, 261, 262, 263, 264, 267, 283, 285
12 Gaba, Christian R., *Scripture of an African People*, Nok N.Y. 1973 64, 122, 257
13 Guillebaud, R., 'The Idea of God in Ruanda-Urundi' in *African Ideas of God* (cf. 33 below) 33 144
14 Harris, W.T., 'The Idea of God among the Mende', 1950 in *African Ideas of God* (cf. 33 below) 33 206
15 Hollis, A.C., *The Nand-Their Language and Folklore*, Oxford 1909 163
16 Idowu, E.B., *Olodumare, God in Yoruba Belief*, London 1962 143, 245, 279
17 Kenyatta, J., *Facing Mount Kenya*, London 1938 31, 204
18 Kenyatta, J., *My people of Kikuyu*, Nairobi 1966 8, 44
19 Konadu, A., *A woman in her prime*, London 1967 45
20 Lindblom, C., *The Akamba of British East Africa*, Uppsala 1920 170
21 Mbiti, John, *The Prayers of African Religion*, SPCK 1975 23, 35, 67, 100, 106, 121, 128, 130, 135, 138, 145, 167, 193, 196, 235, 236, 247, 249
22 Moreau, J., 'Les Pygmées' in *Parole et Mission*, XI, 1960 p. 548, 168
23 di Nola, A.M., *The Prayers of Man*, Heinemann 1962 42, 69, 70, 94, 142, 158, 164, 171, 185, 195, 202, 274

24 Nyom, B., 'Le sacré et l'unité de l'homme', Doctoral Thesis, Lille 1964 68

25 Pawelzik, Fritz, (ed), *I lie on my mat and pray*, Friendship Press 1964 7, 77, 84, 161, 177

26 Pawelzik, Fritz, (ed), *I sing your praises all day long*, Friendship Press 1967 26, 60, 89, 190, 278

27 Poirier, R., Personal collection, Bethel Park, Pennsylvania 15102 n.d. 1, 75, 112, 123, 259

28 Roscoe, J., *The Baktiara or Banyoro*, Cambridge 1923 197

29 Samburu Manuscript Prayers, Consolata Fathers, London n.d. 19, 21, 29, 39, 43, 99, 114, 131, 137, 139, 146, 155, 157, 160, 174, 175, 178, 183, 187, 189, 192, 194, 199, 203, 216, 218, 219, 224, 227, 230, 239, 242, 248, 254, 260, 266, 270, 276, 282

30 Seligman, C.G. and B.Z., *The Pagan Tribes of the Nilotic Sudan*, London 1932 253

31 Shorter, Aylward, 'Divine Call and Human Response' in *The Way* vol 23 nos 1 and 3, 1983 85, 271

32 Shorter, Aylward (ed)., *Prayer in the Religious Traditions of Africa*, Oxford 1975 18, 71, 93, 101, 153, 159, 169, 234, 237, 250, 255, 280

33 Smith, Edwin, W., (ed) *African Ideas of God*, London 1950, 1961 3, 10, 98, 144, 172, 188, 191, 206

34 Sundkler, B., *Bantu Prophets in South Africa*, Oxford, 1948 52

35 Tescaroli, Cirillo, 'Catholic Elite', Oct 1981 273

36 Tutschek, C.A., *Grammar of the Galla (Boran) Language*, Munich 1845 85, 271

37 Westermann, D., *The Shilluk People*, Berlin 1912 277

38 Williams, J.T., *Africa's God*, Boston College Grad School 10 vols 1936-7 265

39 Wilson, M., *Communal Rituals of the Nyakyusa*, Oxford 1959 103, 212

40 Wilson, M., *Rituals of Kinship among the Nyakyusa*, 1957 208

41 Yokoo, S. 'Death among the Abaluyia', Diploma dissertation, Kampala 1966 201

The Holy Bible

Editor's adaptations: 1, 2, 11, 14, 18, 27, 41, 46, 55, 58, 59, 73, 74, 76, 81, 95, 100, 104, 108, 119, 120, 166, 176, 179, 184, 205, 209, 210, 213, 215, 244, 246, 251, 268, 269, 272, 284

Jerusalem Bible: 38, 51, 53, 66, 79, 82, 92, 102, 113, 116, 124, 129, 136, 154, 156, 162, 225, 228, 229, 232, 233, 256
Other 22, 88, 91, 241, 258, 275, 281

*References are to item numbers in this book

Thematic Index

Acknowledgements

The publishers are grateful for permission to reproduce the following from copyright material (for exact references, see Bibliography, p. 171).

Various bible texts, taken from *The Jerusalem Bible*, published and copyright 1966, 1967 and 1968 by Darton Longman and Todd Ltd and Doubleday and Co. Inc.

Texts from *Forms of Prayer, for Jewish Worship, Daily and Sabbath*, edited by the Assembly of Rabbis of the Reform Synagogues of Great Britain © 1977 Reform Synagogues of Great Britain.

Fritz Pawelizik (ed.), *I lie on my mat and pray*, Friendship Press, 1964. *I sing your praises all day long*, Friendhship Press, 1967.

G. Dieterlen (ed.), *Textes sacrés d'Afrique Noire*, Editions Gallimard, 1965.

A.M. di Nola, *The Prayers of Man*, William Heinemann Ltd, 1962.

M. Wilson, *Communal Rituals of the Nyakusa*, published for the International African Institute by Oxford University Press, 1959. Used by permission of the International African Institute.

Aylward Shorter (ed.), *Prayer in the Religious Traditions of Africa*, Oxford University Press East Africa, 1975.

John Mbiti, *The Prayers of African Religion*, SPCK, 1975.

Christian R. Gaba, *Scripture of an African People*, Nok, 1973.